ITALIAN PACKAGING CONTRACTOR

Strange Business Meetings

Fabiano Manzan

I dedicate this book to my two sons, Alan and Francesco, and to all those technicians who are currently testing our lines of automatic machines around the world, as well as to their families from whom they are sometimes away for months.

ACKNOWLEDGMENT

I thank my wife Virginia and my sons Francesco and Alan for their moral support during the writing of this book. I also thank Marta Marelli, Salvatore di Stefano, Renato Perrotti, Carmelo Burgio, Cosimo Salvatore Bianchi, Vittorio Russo, Paola Brienza, Paolo Fogazzi, Davide Andreis, Pierluigi Apollonio, Andrea Piovan.

ABOUT THE AUTHOR

Fabiano Manzan is an electronic engineer specialized in the software development of automatic machine lines in the packaging area, which includes food, tissue, non-food, paper, pharma, cosmetics, etc... After a military experience as a Second Lieutenant in the 185th parachute artillery of the Folgore Brigade, he graduated from the University of Bologna.

He is one of tens of thousands of Italians who travel the world to work as a technician. After 36 years of activity and 64 countries often visited in medium/high-risk areas, Security Manager is certified ISO/UNI 10459

Security Travel Risk UNI/PDR 124/22 update 12.09.2023.

The reason is simple: Many companies, when they send their technicians or salespeople abroad, do not comply with Legislative Decree 81/2008, Legislative Decree. 231/2001 and ISO/UNI 31030, essentially either out of ignorance or to save money.

This entails an enormous risk if the company does not organize the trips (especially in risk areas), preceding them with training courses, information on the country sheets, and drawing up a DVR (risk validation document) which has the aim of eliminating or mitigating the risk which technically is $R=P*I$ where $R=$ Risk, $P=$Probability that a harmful event will occur and $I=$Impact, i.e., the amount of damage.

Insurance is not sufficient as it will pay the stipulated premium only if the company has complied with the 2 laws mentioned above.

TABLE OF CONTENTS

PROLOGUE

Baghdad Hotel, Baghdad, Iraq, March 2, 2021.

I was at the bar of the Baghdad Hotel (Baghdad), which is located on the eastern bank of the Tigris River in front of the "Green Zone," home to the Embassy of the United States of America and various Iraqi Ministries. I was hosted in this hotel during an SAT (Site Approval Test) commissioning of a croissant packaging line for the local company, Al Dalu, on behalf of an Italian company.

In the evening, around 10 pm on March 2, 2021, I was drinking a beer and talking about this and that with the usual Iraqi gentleman who came every evening to drink his daily bottle of whiskey, given that alcohol was flowing at the Baghdad Hotel as well as at the Babylon Hotel in rivers.

Suddenly, someone touched me from behind. I turned; they were three of the Iraqi secret services (who had been keeping an eye on me for a week) in perfect dark suits with ties, earphones, and dark glasses.

They told me in decent English to pack my bags within 15 minutes, and they would transfer me to another hotel for unspecified "security reasons." I didn't ask why!

PREFACE

Having the privilege of presenting the book *"ITALIAN PACKAGING CONTRACTOR,"* a little out of the ordinary, gives me the opportunity to also present the author, who, similar to the writing, appears like a character from other times which fits harmoniously in the modern context where everything happens in a "hybrid" way, particularly in the working world shaped by the globalization of commercial, political and social relationships. The book, organized according to a plot made up of specific stories taken from the work experience of a seasoned and far-sighted professional of a technical-commercial network of on-site services, which have now become necessary and cannot be deferred due to specific peculiarities, highlights very direct and somewhat bizarre "hilarious" important issues of the world of work in non-national contexts. A personal experience that frames aspects and carries out analysis on a larger scale, involving world travelers for any purpose and needs who find themselves immersed in different or completely unknown ethnic realities. Outside national borders, the rules, daily life, culture, ways of doing things, and behaviors are not exactly what we are used to. A natural sign of affection for us can be understood as a lack of respect and even offensive to the other.

Different stories, different cultures, different characters, and different ways of approaching things. A cultural jungle in which civilizations express their right to be. The book, beyond the facts narrated and directly experienced, constitutes a "handbook" of things to do before leaving the streets and stories of our beloved country behind. Things and pictures of situations to keep in mind in order to carry out correct detailed planning, which, if nothing else, highlight aspects and problems to be faced and possibly overcome. It is not an exam to pass, far from being a teacher of life, but a mentor for traveling abroad.

The text begins with stories, memories of professional life, and encounters with individuals from various cultures, histories, and nations, presented with a narrative simplicity reminiscent of the Pomegranate tales. Anecdotes from a cross-section of a different life, "strange," I would dare say, dictated by passion and professional skills. A chain of "hilarious" work events that form a single body of reading and linearity of expression. Impossible to get distracted or stop reading; the episodes envelop us and transport us to those warm, too sandy places of imperturbable and shady, one would say, almost incredible subjects as militia commanders of an unknown world that smack of friendship. The words involve us as exciting and adventurous, damn realistic, and presenting current scenes. At the end of the book, the author completely changes his style of writing, going from the simple linearity of treatment to the rigid patterns of formality, which is really good. Here, he becomes a true master and instructor of the subject covered, complete with legal references and disciplines recalled. The book is, therefore, an adventurous story of lived realities and also a collection of concrete and well-analyzed advice, the result of solid, directly lived work experience. In conclusion, I can state, without fear of being lied to, that the creator of the work has masterfully managed to connect with clear episodes of his work experience abroad, an important reality that concerns every traveler who, for various reasons, must relate to other national realities very different from their own. At the same time, it highlights the age-old problem of coarseness, with which, in our country, important transnational work issues are addressed and directly reflect on the safety and security of our compatriots abroad. I strongly advise all those who intend to travel outside national borders to read carefully or rather to take with them on their travels, this book, which is currently one of a kind because behind the "rhymes and words," there could be personal salvation.

A note for the author: Grande Fabiano, eclectic, adventurous, likeable professional with extensive experience and 360° knowledge, perhaps even a little strange, an Italian who, like few others, writes for the safety and protection of others; BRAVO! –

C.V. VITTORIO RUSSO

(Former Commander Italian Marine Special Forces, GOI)

BOOK PROFILE

In a modern world where manufacturing exports represent a very important sector for Italy, the sector of manufacturers of automatic wrapping and packaging machines continues to improve, growing exponentially from year to year and reaching in 2023 a total turnover of 9 billion and 229 million euros, with an increase of 8% on the previous year (UCIMA data, Union of Automatic Machine Manufacturers). This is the third consecutive record, after that of 2021 and 2022. An important result was achieved, 78.7%, in international markets for a total of 7 billion and 262 million euros and for 21.3%, 1 billion and 967 million euros, in the national one.

In this context, the author analyzes through his personal experience in 36 years of activity, having visited 64 countries abroad, the situation of the so-called "travelers," i.e., technicians and salespeople who go to the most remote places in the world for sales or putting these plants into production, describing what can happen abroad, especially in medium or high-risk geographical areas, moves on to an analysis of the laws in Italy (Legislative Decree 81/2008 and Legislative Decree 231/2001) and the legislation ISO/UNI 31030 provides a summary of what companies should comply with to mitigate or eliminate endogenous and exogenous risks during travel.

Knowing the country's information, habits, and customs of customers favors commercial relations between Italy and these countries.

For this reason, the "traveler" must be informed and trained at the company where he is employed through training courses. Not secondary is the security part carried out through PSC companies (private security companies), which, at present, Italian legislation does not provide for.

Consequently, if an Italian company needs a PSC for its travel workers, it must necessarily turn to one registered abroad. The United States of America and Great Britain absorbs 70% of the world market (total turnover of more than 200 billion USD) with 2 negative effects on us.

The first is that these PSC companies will pay taxes abroad and not in Italy.

The second is that they will have in their hands all the technical-commercial information that they can clearly pass on to the "intelligence agencies" of their country and consequently to our foreign competitors.

CHAPTER 1

From the North-East to the "Packaging Valley" in Emilia Romagna

After graduating from the University of Bologna and fueled by a passion for programming automated machines in the "packaging" and "beverage" sectors, I decided to move permanently to the city. At that time, and still today, it represents the global hub for the construction of these machines.

The "packaging" sector (construction of machinery for packaging food, tissue, paper, non-food, cosmetic, tobacco, pharma) and "beverage" (machinery for filling bottles, bottles for food and non-food liquids) in Italy has a total turnover of around ten billion Euro and employs around 60,000 people (data from U.C.I.M.A. Union of Italian Automatic Machine Manufacturers) among employees and external workers and thanks to our craftsmanship we are the first in the world in terms of turnover and quality.

There is no assembly line in this sector because each machine has its own story; they are all machines made to measure for the customer in question, which is what the Anglo-Saxons call "tailored."

The exports of this sector abroad are around 85%.

Statistically, approximately 10-12% of employees and external workers who work in these two sectors are constantly traveling abroad.

Therefore, we are talking about around 7,000 people who are simultaneously abroad on rotation at various construction sites for the installation of these lines. Generally, the team for testing these machines abroad is composed, in the most complex cases, of mechanics, electricians, and programmers. I have always been attracted to the programming of these machines, and I have always worked as what is commonly called a "software engineer."

I was hired by BFB Spa of Bentivoglio (BO) in 1990 after graduating in electronic engineering in Bologna.

One of the two partners of the company told me, "We need to automate our machines with servomotors, and we hired you for this!"

Therefore, I began to study how to apply servomotors in the various movements that, until that time, were performed by mechanical cams.

Clearly, I came to the conclusion that to make a servomotor create a motion profile, it was first necessary to design a function, that is, a mathematical "master-slave" relationship where the "master" was the old mechanical axis moved by a simple AC motor (alternating current) and an "inverter." At the same time, the "slave" was the old mechanical cam, which would be replaced by servomotors.

At this point, I needed software where I could write the mathematical relationship of the master-slave position with its derivatives (speed and acceleration), and I would do a first "offline" test.

It was 1990 when Windows 3.1 was launched from DOS by writing "WIN" and pressing the "Enter" key.

The most immediate thing was to use the window "Excel" program, which allowed, once the master-slave mathematical function had been written, to display the curve, check any points of discontinuity and its progress, and optimize it.

So I went to my electrical office manager asking to purchase the "Excel" program.

Precisely in those days, the company management forced him to learn to use a computer (he had always refused, considering it unnecessary, let's say, an old-fashioned electrical expert).

One day, they saw him struggling with his new computer, unable to make it work.

He called me telling me that the "contraption" wouldn't work, even though he had been told that in order to launch the Windows program, he had to write "WIN" and press the "Enter" key. He told me he had been trying it for half an hour but still couldn't get it to work.

Not knowing the English language, he had typed "UIN" –that was my boss!

So, not understanding what "Excel" software that I had proposed was for, he told me that the program was not needed by the company (of course, something that you don't understand isn't needed!)

On my initiative, I bought the basic "office" package, which included "Excel "and "Word" and something else, spending half a month's salary and installing it on the company PC that I used in the company.

One day, while I was designing motorcycle profiles using "Excel," the electrical manager noticed and made me uninstall it, stating that I couldn't install software on a company PC that wasn't purchased by the company itself (and rightly so). So why didn't he buy it?

Obviously, I changed company a few years later. I was hired at PRB S.r.l., where I met the legendary engineer Andrea Cinotti, head of the technical office, who was the progenitor of the application of servomotors on tissue machines.

At the end of the 80s, he created a prototype of a packaging machine for toilet paper rolls, a "bundle," replacing the twenty mechanical cams with as many servomotors as possible. In recent years, no one believed it was possible to achieve this. It was a bit like saying today that an automatic machine could be created to operate entirely independently without the need for an operator.

The machine was a success. Unlike the classic mechanical cam version, which required physically replacing cams to change recipes, this new design allowed for recipe changes in just a few minutes. Each product with different dimensions needed different operating data, which could be set quickly via the HMI operator panel, compared to the several hours required for the cam version.

The engineer Cinotti paved the way for the current fully servo-assisted automatic packaging machines with automatic recipe change from HMI (human interface).

Learning that I had already used Allen Bradley programming software called GML (graphical motion language), he told me to "dust it off" and start writing a project.

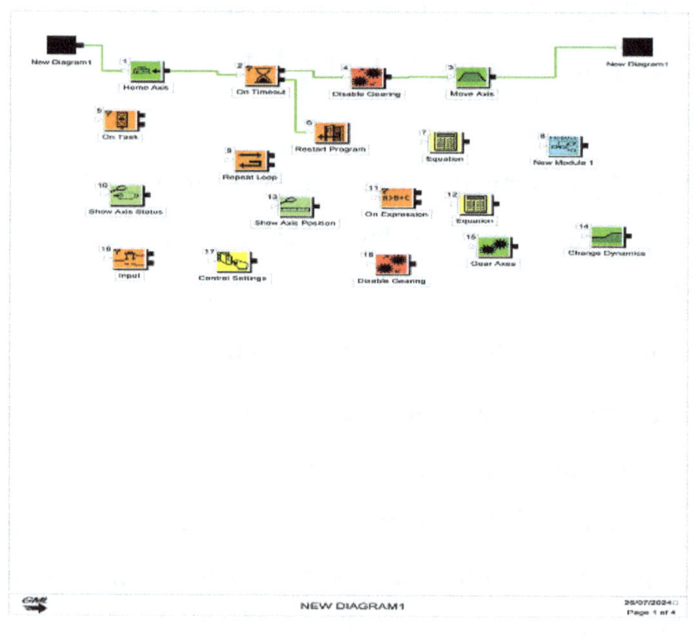

GML (Graphical motion logic) program example

The GML was a very efficient icon-based software for its time.

One day, while I was creating a program, the general manager of the company and partner, a civil engineer, came to my office, looked at my computer screen, made a strange face, and immediately afterwards, his secretary called me to his office.

I went in and asked if I could sit, but he said no and made me wait ten minutes while he looked at some documents.

Then, speaking in an altered tone of voice, he told me that he was very disappointed with how I was behaving as he had seen that I was using the computer with "games" during working hours.

He had mistaken the icons of the "Graphical motion language" software for a game!

I told him to wait five minutes because I would go and call engineer, Cinotti. I found him in his office and told him that the general manager wanted to talk to him about the new icon software and offer him compliments. I arrived at the director's office with engineer Cinotti, and he began to praise all the advantages of the new software.

The director, realizing he had made a mistake, dismissed us in a hurry, and I popped my head out the door and told him. "Doctor, today we beat up a lot of shit."

Clearly, I resigned after a few months; evidently, I wasn't cut out to be an employee!

I opened a VAT number and started my own business.

There was no shortage of clients, and in 34 years, I made hundreds of trips to 64 different countries (the UN recognizes around 198 if I remember correctly, so I visited around a third of them for work).

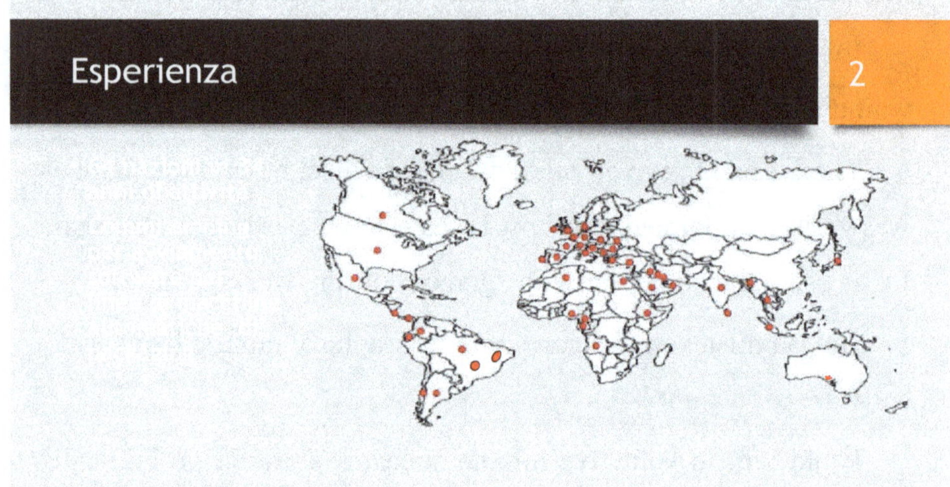

CHAPTER 2

Baghdad, Iraq February 2021

It all started in October 2020.

I was testing a croissant packaging line. As mentioned previously, I specialize in software development, testing, and commissioning for lines in food, non-food, tissue, paper, pharma, and fragrance industries. In short, everything that people buy in supermarkets/shops etc. Now, everything is packaged, sometimes in a way that is too complex.

For example, if you buy bread at the supermarket, you will first have to take one of those paper bags, introduce the bread, and weigh it by choosing the number on the scale's keyboard.

Have you noticed that the bag has a transparent polypropylene window so the cashier can check the type of bread inside? Since scales today aren't equipped with AI (artificial intelligence) to recognize whether you've put in €6/kg bread but pressed the €2.5/kg sandwich button (assuming sandwiches are still sold at that price), the result is that when the bag needs to be discarded, you're supposed to separate the paper from the polypropylene (plastic). And who does that? Nobody!

Every time we have to throw a wrapper that has different components (plastic, paper, aluminum) in the garbage, we are seized by existential crises, thinking of the Green Party or the two champions of AVS (Alleanza Verdi Sinistra), namely Bonelli and Frantoianni, champions of "green deal" who knows what they will think of me?

Having said that, let's go back to the testing of this line of croissants, which went according to plan and the timing agreed upon with the customer.

Looking at the so-called "machine data sheet," a document where everything is written regarding the characteristics of the machine and the customer's requests, type of product, production speed, tolerances of the product itself, name of the customer and country, I see that the end customer is located in Baghdad, Iraq.

Clearly, after a few days, the two owners of the company I was working for arrived and, with a broad twist of words, asked if my presence would be necessary during the SAT (Site Acceptance Test) at the client's location in Baghdad. In contrast, the FAT (Factory Acceptance Test) is conducted by the manufacturer, sometimes involving the end customer either in person or online.

I asked when the departure date would be, and the answer was the evening of January 2, 2021, at 8.20 pm, with arrival on the morning of January 3 at 4.20 am in Baghdad with a Turkish Airlines flight with a stopover in Istanbul.

I didn't immediately respond to their request and told them that I would contact them the following day to give them an answer.

Returning to the hotel, I began to do what "intelligence" experts call OSINT (open source intelligence), that is, a search for information from open sources (internet, newspapers, TV, radio, periodicals...), given that the company had not even worried about the situation I might encounter in Baghdad.

Indeed, to my question, "What situation will I encounter in Baghdad, the answer was, "All is calm; ISIS has now been eradicated."

I started to do my research and tried to understand the current situation in Iraq and recent years.

Synopsis: On September 11, 2001, Al Qaeda hijacked four planes, extended the 2 towers in New York, attacked the Pentagon, and another plane fell in Pennsylvania. February 2002 invasion of Afghanistan, given that Al-Qaida had bases in this country, and the following year, March 2003, after sustained propaganda where Saddam Hussein was described as having weapons of mass destruction, I remember that the American Minister of Defense Colin Powel (RIP) in a press conference in front of journalists from all over the world, shaking vials which he claimed contained anthrax (probably it was tomato sauce which I also produce from my garden) his dramatic presentation scared the whole world by saying that these vials containing this infectious substance were coming via mail from Iraq and could cause millions of deaths in the United States and allied countries.

International observers were sent for months to establish whether Iraq had these weapons of mass destruction (atomic bombs, projectiles that released gases, chemical or biological substances, etc., upon their explosion). What they found after arduous searches were a few half-empty cylinders of cooking gas.

US President George W. Bush did not learn the lesson from his father, George H. W. Bush, who led the first Gulf War. If you invade a country, the first rule is not to completely eradicate its armed forces. You can remove some generals and perhaps some colonels, but what happens if you entirely disintegrate an army?

Essentially two things:

o What will the soldiers, from the lowest ranks to the generals, do next? What will they live on? Can hundreds of thousands of people who have always worked in the military suddenly transition to civilian life?

o Suppose a nation finds itself without an army and police. In that case, it suddenly causes chaos, and you have to rebuild everything, so you will need some former commanders, for example, who know the customs and habits of the locals.

So Iraq was invaded, the army was destroyed, the air force had already been eliminated during the first Gulf War, and the "no-fly zone" was already present on the northern and southern borders of Iraq since the first Gulf War. This led to a state of total chaos.

In 2004, ISIS was born out of "nowhere" (which are Sunni former supporters of Saddam Hussein, probably financed by Saudi Arabia, Arab Emirates, and Qatar), unlike the vast majority of lower middle-class Iraqis who are Shiites.

Even within what was the Iraqi army, the senior officers were all Sunnis, while the lower officers, non-commissioned officers, and troops were Shiites.

Coming down from the North, ISIS reached the gates of Baghdad.

The former Iraqi soldiers asked the Americans for weapons to fight ISIS, and the Americans refused, but Iran fully supported this initiative. Pro-Iran Shiite militias are created, such as the Kataib Hezbollah, Kataib Al Iman Ali, Asaib Ahl al Haq, and the Badr group, among others.

All these militias coalesced in 2014 into the PMF (Popular Mobilization Forces) led by Abu Mahdi Al Muhandis.

Therefore, the international coalition led by the USA and other nations, including Italian participation along with what little remained of the Iraqi army and all the various Shiite militias financed by Shiite Iran, fought against ISIS and defeated it in 2017 in the two battles of Mosul (although largely defeated, ISIS continued to smolder under the ashes on the borders with Syria).

Once the ISIS problem was over, the PMF, with the various militias, began the so-called "Muqawama," i.e., resistance against the United States and their allies (especially Turkey).

The concept of "muqawama" is the basis of all Shiite militias, interpreted as resistance against the oppressor, i.e., the foreign occupying forces.

In the Middle Eastern area, pro-Iranian militias tend to consider the borders between Iraq, Syria, and Lebanon as structures imposed by Westerners. For this reason, they often operated transnationally, although maintaining very strong local rivalries and interests.

The Popular Mobilization Forces are now recognized as part of the Iraqi state security forces. The various militias provide specific battalions to the country's army, thus maintaining relations with the central government. Many of their militiamen are paid as soldiers of the army, and their commanders often have command positions in the same way. At the same time, the militias guarantee themselves a certain freedom of action, as confirmed by the recent attacks on US positions, which the Iraqi government does not approve of, at least officially.

Kataib Hezbollah is one of the largest of these militias, numbering 20-30 thousand men.

Founded in 2003 and has been defined as a terrorist organization by the United States since 2009, it has carried out attacks with rockets, firearms, and car bombs. Currently, it also possesses drones and short-range missiles of Iranian origin. It was led by Abu Mahdi al Muhandis, who was killed in January 2020 by the American attack, which had as its main objective the Iranian general Qassem Soleimani, considered one of the main architects of the policy of Iranian influence through armed militias.

It is also common to other Iraqi militias, such as Asaib Ahl al Haq and the Badr group, which are considered rivals for reasons of recruitment, prestige, and operational choices. However, Kataib Hezbollah shares a common inspiration and Shiite financing.

Between 31 December 2019 and 1 January 2020, there was a huge demonstration in Baghdad and the demonstrators near the "Green Zone," supported by the militiamen of Kataib Hezbollah, Kataib Al Iman Ali, and in general by the Popular Mobilization Forces (PMF) along with supporters, sympathizers attacked the US embassy in the "Green Zone" in response to US airstrikes on Iraq and Syria in 2019 that killed 25 people and injured 55 Kataib Hezbollah fighters.

The attack occurred in the context of the 2019-2020 Persian Gulf crisis, leading the United States of America to blame Iran and its allies in Iraq for orchestrating the embassy attack. The United States responded by sending hundreds of additional troops to the Persian Gulf region between Iraq and Kuwait, including about a hundred U.S. Marines, to bolster security at the Baghdad embassy. No deaths or serious injuries occurred among Americans during the attack, and protesters never breached the main compound.

Attack on the US Embassy 31 December 2019-1 January 2020

Billboards in Baghdad praising Abu Madi Al Muhandis and Qasem
Soleimani

But coming back to us, what immediately caught my eye were these huge billboards all over Baghdad praising Mayor General Qasem Soleimani and Abu Madis Al Muhandis as head of the PMF (Popular Mobilization Force).

Exactly one year prior (compared to my arrival date in Baghdad proposed by the Italian company, on the night between 2 and 3 January 2020), Abu Mahdi Al Muhandis went with his escort to Baghdad airport; they entered and received Qasem Soleimani, chief of Iran's Quds Forces and its security escort of five Iranians.

Mayor General Qassen Soleimani, short in stature and notoriously shy, was the head of the elite team for the most secret operations and, above all, a key man in the Ayatollah's regime. In the last twenty years before his death, the general had gained almost mythical fame among both his enemies and many Iraqi supporters. In fact, he was the most influential figure in Iran after President Ali Khamenei.

I remember that we are in the middle of the Covid era in the Middle East, while in Italy, we were beginning to see a slight decline. Qasem Soleimani took a commercial flight from Tehran naturally under a false name (face partially covered by the anti-covid mask), made a connection in Damascus (Syria), and landed with his escort in Baghdad at 00.20 on 3 January.

Abu Mahdi Al Muhandis receives him at the plane's steps (I really don't think he went through customs or passport control), and the convoy of 2 armored SUVs with 5 Iranians and 5 Iraqis on board leaves the airport following the road that turns in a U-shape heading north-east towards Baghdad.

Aerial photo of Baghdad airport with a semi-ring exiting towards the center of Baghdad.

Previously, the news of Qasem Soleimani's trip had probably reached the American services via the Israeli services. American President Donald Trump, Qasem Soleimani's bitter enemy, was informed of the fact, and he gave the order (without consulting Congress) to take off 3 MQ Reaper-9 drones with 2 Hellfire missiles each on board (each missile has 40 kg of high explosive). Furthermore, an APACHE helicopter also took off as a plan B in case the drones failed in the attack.

Drone MQ Reaper-9

Attack helicopter Apache

This type of drone flies at a service altitude (ready to attack) of 7,500 m, guided via satellite from thousands of km away with very high-resolution infrared cameras, using facial recognition software to identify a person several kilometers away.

Probably as the convoy passed near the airport, there was some reconnaissance and target acquirer on the ground who was "illuminating" the target of the two SUVs with a laser as the Hellfire missile is much more precise if in the latter so-called "mile" follows a pointing laser.

Classic communication from the central command to the acquisition operator "LASER ON" targets, and 2 missiles were launched, one for each SUV.

This decision was later openly contested by Nancy Pelosi, who was speaker of the American Parliament, describing the action as a premeditated murder that would have further destabilized the Iraqi situation and so it was.

Furthermore, on the following day, January 4, 2020, in a further targeted attack carried out in the Taji area, north of Baghdad, the head of the Katai'b Hezbollah brigades (a pro-Iranian Iraqi Shiite paramilitary group), the general secretary Shibl al -Zaydi. His brother and four other people were killed in the attack.

So, if my arrival in Baghdad had been, as proposed by the company, on January 3, 2021, I would have found myself between two people and not a commemoration!

Result of the 2 Hellfire missiles on the convoy leaving Baghdad airport.

The attack of the two Hellfire missiles was so precise, causing 5 Iranian and 5 Iraqi deaths, that only the following morning at 06.30 was there confirmation that Qasem Soleimani had also died because they found his famous ring with his finger attached.

Following this attack on Iraqi territory on the night between 2 and 3 January 2020, I concluded that there was no point in going to Baghdad exactly one year later.

My prediction was accurate, as on January 3, 2021, there were huge demonstrations with a related attempt at a further attack on the American embassy in Baghdad.

I proposed a flight from Venice on February 11th with a connection to Istanbul, the final destination Baghdad, and arrival on February 12th.

I explicitly asked for a flight that arrived in Baghdad in the early hours of the morning. I chose the Turkish Airlines flight TK802, arriving at 04.20 on February 12th, a time that was not random as, according to my calculations, after about an hour of completing customs formalities, I could get to travel from the airport to the factory before 06.00.

The reason is simple: when traveling with an escort, it is always better to avoid the chaotic traffic of Baghdad as it is not very healthy to remain in a queue with two escort SUVs easily recognizable by their armor with two live M4 or AK47s sticking out of the windows, some might wonder who's inside!

At the Venice airport, at the hand baggage check, they made me take off my desert boots. While I was putting them back on, one of the three Guardia di Finanza operators almost always positioned themselves in that area before the duty-free approached.

He asked me for my passport and boarding pass, and seeing that the final destination was Baghdad, he became curious and asked me the reason for the trip.

I replied that I was a software engineer and that I was going to test a croissant production and packaging line in Baghdad.

Then, the non-commissioned officer, thinking I was joking, asked me for a document that proved what I was saying.

I showed him the invitation letter from the Iraqi customer, and he nodded in approval, saying, "I didn't think Iraqis ate croissants, too."

Answer: "They eat them empty or filled with cream or jam, exactly like us."

I arrived in Istanbul at 11.40 pm local time and connected to Baghdad at 01.20 am, where we landed at 04.20 am with an Airbus A330-203, which had 268 seats.

At least a hundred of these were occupied by individuals with beards and long hair, tattooed, with military-style backpacks as cabin baggage, certainly not going to Baghdad on holiday.

There were Americans, English, Spaniards, Poles, and even some Italians... clearly contractors.

Upon arrival at the airport in Baghdad, they separated the passengers with Iraqi passports from the others. Those with Iraqi passports went through the checks very quickly while the others, including me, were put in a large room waiting for the office that issued the entry visa to open.

To visit Iraq, it is sufficient to have an "invitation letter" from an Iraqi company or a private resident in Iraq upon check-in at the airport of departure, and the visa is issued on-site upon payment of 80 USD in cash (they do not disdain not even the 80 EUR which is worth a little more than the 80 USD, but they didn't accept credit cards) and they issued a regular receipt written in Arabic.

They informed me that the visa issuing office would open at 08.00, so I patiently waited for it to open.

After about 15 minutes, I heard someone call my name. I approached, and a young man introduced himself by identifying himself with his identity card. His name was Rami.

I told him I spoke on the phone with Abu Rami and asked if he was his relative. (Abu Rami was the owner of the "close protection" company that would escort me on the airport-factory journey).

He replied, "Abu Rami is my father. I am here to help you complete the paperwork for entry into Iraq."

Curiosity: In Arabic-speaking countries, a father often adopts the suffix ABU (father of) as his nickname, combined with the name of his firstborn. Therefore, Rami (son) becomes Abu Rami (father of Rami).

Another famous Iraqi ABU is Abu Azrael, which means father of the angel of death (the picturesque name he gave to his firstborn son), but I will talk to you about this ABU later.

Rami, who was in the passport control area (I'm not sure how he had the authorization to be there, as it is normally restricted to those disembarking from international flights or airport officials), approached the office door and pounded on it until the visa official appeared, still half-asleep. Seeing Rami, the official let us in, apologizing and issuing my visa within five minutes. Afterward, he closed the door, and I went back to sleep, probably until the office's official opening at 08:00, while the rest of the passengers continued to wait.

Having the right connection makes things quick!

Visa issued upon arrival at Baghdad airport

After leaving the passport control area amidst the general grumbling of the hundred contractors and other passengers,

Outside the airport, an armed escort was waiting for me composed of a "team leader" (Bosnian), a "second in charge," and two Iraqi "drivers," the classic composition of a CPT (close protection team) of a PSC (private security company).).

In Iraq, the team leader of a "close protection team" is never Iraqi but always an expatriate (EXPAT). In my case, the Bosnian expatriate was so big that the bulletproof vest looked like a bib.

"Close Protection Team" made up of an Expat and three Iraqis.

Putting yourself in the hands of four Iraqis is never a good idea; given that they generally earn much less than the team leader, some bad ideas could pop into their heads.

What I mean is that if someone wants to kidnap you, your value is directly proportional to the importance of the company you are working for.

The "close protection team" provided under the contract had the following characteristics at a cost of $1,200 per day. I was informed that a few years earlier, when ISIS was almost in Baghdad, the cost had risen to $3,500 per day.

SERIAL	POST	FUNCTION	TOTAL	ON	TOTAL	TOTAL	TOTAL	ROTATI	FEE USD
2 x B6 SUV LC with Exp.TL & LN 2IC									
1	MCPTTL- Mobile Close Protection Team Leader Armed (Expatriate)	MCPT TL – Mobile Close Protection Team Leader Qualified: - Minimum 5 years' military background - SIA Certificate -Criminal Disclosure Certificate -FPOSI Medical qualification or accredited equivalent	1		On duty = standby when not on-mission	On duty = standby when not on a mission	-	According to DAR Rotation	Ad Hoc PSD Team / $1,200 / day Monthly Rate / $32,000

	-Accredited Close Protection course *-Previous relevant experience*						
MCPT2I/C - Mobile Close Protection Team Second-in-Charge Armed (Local National)	*MCPT 2iC – Second-in-Charge.* *-Minimum 5 years' military background* *-Criminal Disclosure Certificate* *-FPOSI Medical qualification or accredited equivalent* *-Accredite*	*1*					

		d Close Protection course -Previous relevant experience							
	MCPTB6SUV – Mobile Close Protection Team B6 Armored Vehicle Driver/ Operative Armed (Local National)	Qualified B6 armored car driver and close protection operative. - Minimum 2 years *of* Close Protection / Military / Police experience -MOI Criminal Disclosure Certificate -Basic Medical Training	2						

		- Reasonable English speaking and understanding -Medical – Fit for work. -Driving License – or applied For. -Bilingual & Literate English / Arabic					

They made me wear the usual bulletproof vest, and we set off along the half-ring out of the airport, heading east towards the center of Baghdad.

After about 1 km, I noticed that the road had huge, roughly patched potholes, and there were dozens of bunches of flowers on the sides.

Precisely there, a year earlier, the Americans had eliminated Qasem Soleimani and Abu Mahdi Al Muhandis together with their escorts by launching two Hellfire missiles.

After about another kilometre, the convoy of 2 SUVs pulled up behind another...

I thought, what now?

This was technically a "support" SUV that supplies weapons and ammunition to the escort since "officially' one cannot enter the "buffer zone" of about two kilometers around the airport armed; in fact, anyone arriving by taxi at the airport is stopped, checked with the underbody mirror, engine compartment and trunk opened, searched, made to get out and forced to take one of the taxis parked near this checkpoint.

When I arrived at the factory, the first thing I noticed was that it seemed like entering a barracks, three-meter meter-high walls with a fence on top along the four sides of the perimeter, four garrisons with men armed with AK47s, and a couple of armed operators patrolling the surrounding wall day and night.

One side of the factory bordered Baghdad's largest electricity generation plant.

Baghdad airport entrance street

I came up with some basic rules when going to these types of high-risk countries: stay away from:

1- Sensitive sites (power, gas, nuclear power plants)

2- Do not tailgate convoys of the armed forces/police (they may be subject to terrorist attacks).

3- Ports and airports.

4- Barracks

5- Various events

6- Don't travel on roads that are suddenly traffic-free when they normally are.

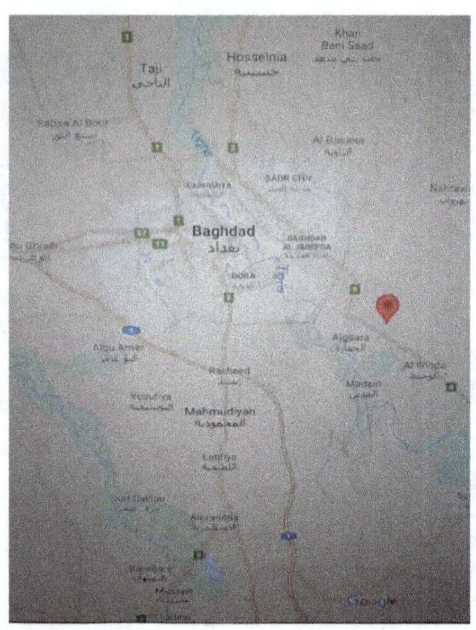

Location of the AL-Dalu Factory approximately 20 km south-east of Baghdad

The factory bordered this power plant, and since I couldn't move one of the two, I resigned.

My fears, however, were not unfounded as I received news that, two months after my return to Italy, following the frequent lack of electricity in Baghdad, a few tens of thousands of people arrived from the city center to protest about the lack of electricity.

They tried to attack the Besmaya city power plant, and there were heavy clashes with the police, with 3-4 deaths hit by the police "AMVI" (High Mobility Multipurpose Wheeled Vehicle).

The demonstrators were stopped on the access road to the power plant but tried to enter the factory and then climb over the wall bordering the power plant.

Clearly, if I had been in the factory with my PC on the production line, calmly programming the machines, they certainly would not have asked me kindly to move, but I certainly would have been involved in the clashes.

They were unable to enter the factory perimeter because factory security began firing M4s and AK47s into the air, and the protesters gave up.

As per the contractual agreements, the customer had to provide me with a "compound" in the factory for my stay and provide me with three daily meals.

The same day, they took me to a medical center for the Covid 19 test, where I tested negative.

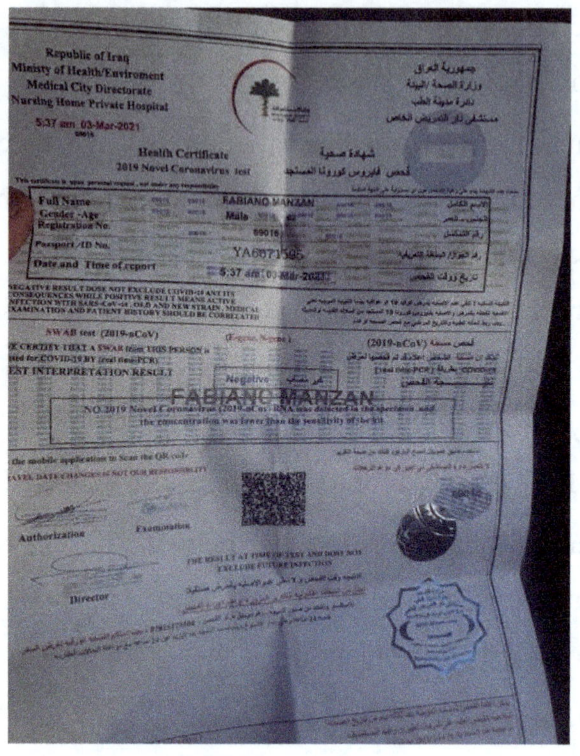

Test result covid-19

A few months earlier, the customer had sent an email guaranteeing all this with attached photos of the "compound."

The photos were of some hotel rooms, but I found a dirty room in front of me, with clogged toilets and sheets that had seen better times.

One day I asked if they could buy me some beers, they arrived with two boxes, after five minutes a counter order arrived and they took them away, after half an hour they brought them back, who understands them?

As for the meals in the midst of the Covid era, they consisted of a plate of rice with pieces of chicken or lamb, and I ate them at the same table with 3 other factory employees who punctually arrived from the production line, went to the bathroom but couldn't wash their hands as the sink was also always clogged.

Clearly following their habits and customs, they ate with their hands. At most, you could eat with a piece of Arab bread (similar to a Romagna piadina, so to speak).

Since there were always four of us, I thought everyone would limit themselves to their quarter of the plate, but the choices of rice mixed with chicken or lamb were completely random, even in my sector.

Clearly, out of respect for local habits and customs, I participated by demonstrating a "strong enthusiasm" for their way of eating.

After my return to Italy, two of these feasters were informed that they had died due to a lung infection caused by Covid!

I was lucky as hell. I never got it despite having traveled for work in the Covid era, Angola, Vietnam, Colombia, Cameroon, etc., but it's just a matter of luck.

Of course, after a couple of days, I sent an email to the factory owner and my client in Italy requesting a transfer to a decent hotel. They accepted, but the problem was that in the meantime, Baghdad had entered a curfew due to Covid. The only people who could go around were the police, army, and militia operators; not even the various PSCs (private security companies) had a permit to operate (this was what they told me in the factory; in reality, they probably wanted to save on supplies).

The factory owner told me this would not be a problem as he would have me escorted daily by his "security manager," his trusted man responsible for the factory's safety.

A rather thin person showed up in the office, to whom we will give the name of Mr Abu, with a classic Middle Eastern beard and moustache, eyes that had seen many years of war, dressed in a desert vegetative military uniform, desert boot, armed with an M4, a Glock pistol and 9 magazines in the 5.56 mm caliber cartridge cases, I noticed that the safety of the M4 was on so he usually had a round in the chamber just in case.

Mr. Abu was limping and told me in understandable English that an ISIS fighter had wounded him in the second battle of Mosul.

The exact words were, "A fucking ISIS shot me in Mosul." *Let's start well,* I thought.

He brought me a military jacket of my size, which was at least 3 sizes larger than his, and told me that I would have to wear it every time we made the morning journey from the hotel to the factory and vice versa in the evening (a journey of about 20 km).

He told me it was to avoid being so conspicuous. As you can see here, almost everyone is dressed like this.

Mr. Abu and I before a transfer from the factory to the hotel.

Mr. Abu was armed with an M4 and Glock during the escort

We had to choose the hotel where I would stay, and they gave me three options: Palestine Hotel, Babylon Rotana Hotel, or Baghdad Hotel.

Palestine Hotel (Baghdad)

Babylon Rotana Hotel (Baghdad)

Baghdad Hotel (Baghdad)

We started with the Palestine Hotel. We went to the reception, but despite being new and huge, it was squalid. What struck me was that the only guest was me!

Mindful of the advice to avoid normally crowded places that have suddenly become deserted, I declined the accommodation offer.

We went to the Babylon Rotana Hotel on the east bank of the Tigris River opposite the "Green Zone," home to almost all foreign embassies and Iraqi ministries.

It was a beautiful five-star hotel with a small problem: it was full of "contractors" of various nationalities, especially Americans and English. I thought it was better to stay away; you never know if someone mistakes me for one of them. I'm a "contractor, but for automatic croissant packaging machines," which is another type of contractor.

In the meantime, I received a phone call from the Italian company where someone monitored my movements via WhatsApp "location in real-time," asking me where I was going. I replied: "to look for a hotel since the factory compound is unlivable!"

On our third trip, we arrived at the third hotel, the Baghdad Hotel, on the east bank of the Tigris river, with the usual "Green zone" on the west side.

We arrived at the hotel checkpoint (all the most important hotels are protected by a "Buffer zone" in order to limit damage from possible car bombs), where Mr. Abu left the M4 carbine and the Glock pistol in custody, and we entered the reception.

The scene was very funny. Entering the reception of a 4-star hotel, where elegant men were accompanied by equally fashionable ladies in stiletto heels and Mr. Abu, in a military suit and desert boots, felt like stepping into a movie. Moreover, I noticed that Mr. Abu was well-known and highly respected by the hotel staff.

Mr. Abu had previously called and had already booked a room; I registered, and I asked for a west side room for a very simple reason: the probability of an attacker with a portable rocket launcher throwing a grenade towards the hotel was much lower from the west side where there is the "green zone" which is "off limits."

Mr. Abu paid for about twenty days in cash and greeted me by telling me that he would wait for me the next morning at the reception at 07.00.

I thanked him, carried my suitcase and trolley, and took the lift.

The doors opened, but it was full; four men and a woman who spoke English with a strong Italian-Roman accent told me it was full.

I replied: "I see that the elevator is busy; please go. I will take the next one".

They clearly understood from the accent that I was Italian and asked me for confirmation.

The room was very comfortable, with a terrace facing the "green zone" with the American Embassy about 1 km away.

As I always do, I requested a room on an intermediate floor—not too low (which could be risky in case of a terrorist attack) and not too high (since knotted sheets might not be sufficient for an emergency escape from the window).

Dinner time arrived, and I went to the restaurant. While ordering dinner, a few dozen Italians arrived (I remained vague intentionally), including some women.

I thought they were obviously not on a tourist trip to Baghdad. Some had overalls with a patch. I looked closer; they were from the Vatican State Gendarmerie Corps.

I remembered that the Holy Father would arrive in Baghdad to visit the Grand Ayatollah of Baghdad Al Sistani on March 5th, so their presence before the pastoral visit of the Holy Father was normal.

Vatican State Gendarmerie Corps

Welcome of the Iraqi people to the Holy Father

Iraqi and Vatican flag

Guard of honor awaiting the arrival of the Holy Father

The arrival of the Holy Father at the airport in Baghdad

The Holy Father visits Grand Ayatollah Al Sistani.

- The Vatican Gendarmerie Corps arrives a few weeks in advance at the place where the Holy Father's visit will take place, and among its tasks is to carry out the so-called "reclamation," that is, to secure the route, rest areas, premises of meetings, etc.

- Some may confuse the Vatican Gendarmerie with the Swiss Guards.

- Just to clarify, the Gendarmerie Corps of the Vatican City State, informally the Vatican Gendarmerie, is a surveillance body, dependent on the Governorate of the Vatican City State, responsible for ensuring public order, as well as carrying out intelligence functions, judicial and road traffic surveillance police in the territory of the Vatican City State and its numerous extraterritorial areas.

Within the Vatican Gendarmerie, there are the following ranks:

- *Official role:* with the ranks of deputy commissioner, commissioner, first manager, senior manager (officers), general manager, inspector general (general officers).

- *Non-Commissioned Officers role:* with the ranks of vice-brigadier, brigadier (non-commissioned officers), sub-inspector, and inspector (senior non-commissioned officers).

- *Troop role:* with the ranks of pupil and gendarme

- Individuals with Italian or Vatican citizenship, male, unmarried, with a high school diploma, aged between 21 and 24 years old, and no less than 1.80 m tall can aspire to enlist in the gendarmerie. In addition to the psychophysical suitability for the tasks to be carried out and the use of weapons, it is necessary to profess and practice the Catholic faith. This characteristic must be proven by a letter of introduction from one's parish priest or a prelate, which ensures the interested party's serious knowledge, even religion.

- *The Pontifical Swiss Guard (also called Swiss Guard; in Latin*: Pontificia Cohors Helvetica or Cohors Pedestris Helvetiorum a Sacra Custodia Pontificis; in German: Päpstliche Schweizergarde; in French: Garde suisse pontificale is an armed body to protect the Pope and his residence, created on 22 January 1506. It is the only Swiss Guard corps still operational and is the oldest permanent corps in the world to have been in service for over five centuries without interruption.

- He serves in Vatican City during the Pope's travels with security agents.

- The typical colored Renaissance-style uniform for solemn ceremonies is accompanied by more sober clothing at an operational level.

- The modern Guard has the role of personal defense of the pontiff. The Papal Swiss Guard is formally equipped with traditional weapons such as halberds, but all guards also have modern portable firearms.

- Since the attempted assassination of John Paul II in 1981, the Swiss Guard has been oriented from the traditional role heavily conditioned by ceremonial to a more active role in the defense of the person of the Pope.

- The recruits of this corps must necessarily be Swiss citizens, Catholic, male between 19 and 30 years old, and must have completed a period of training in the Swiss army.

- The arrival of the Holy Father was scheduled for March 5 with the arrival at Baghdad airport and also a visit to the personal residence of Ali al-Husayni al-Sistani (in Arabic

علي الحسيني السيستاني, born on 4 August 1930, one of the most senior Twelver Shia scholars with the rank of Grand Ayatollah, spiritual leader of Shia Muslims throughout the Islamic world and is the undisputed leader of Iraqi Shia.

- Among other things, "Time magazine" described him in 2004 and 2005 as one of the 100 most influential people in the world.

- The character is so important to give an idea that when he receives any civil, military, or religious authority at his home, he never gets up from his chair, and vice versa. When the Holy Father arrived, he got up and embraced him.

- There has always been a link between the PMF (Popular Mobilization Forces) and Ayatollah Ali Al-Sistani.

- The PMF is an Iraqi state security service that Iran has infiltrated and used to exert significant influence in Iraq. Iran's co-optation of the PMF allows Tehran to pursue its objectives in Iraq while obscuring its actual involvement in Iraqi internal affairs.

- Understanding how Iranian leaders exert direct and indirect influence over this significant component of Iraq's security sector is crucial as the United States considers how to deter Iranian-backed Iraqi militias from attacking U.S. forces in Iraq and Syria.

The PMF began as part of the effort to halt and reverse the advance of the Islamic State of Iraq and Al-Sham (ISIS) from Syria into Iraq but has largely become a front for militias responding to Iran.

Former Iraqi Prime Minister Nouri al Maliki formed the PMF in June 2014 by "institutionalizing" pre-existing, predominantly Shia militias that were engaged in the fight against ISIS.

ISIS captured Mosul in June 2014, prompting prominent Iraqi Shiite cleric Grand Ayatollah Ali Al-Sistani to issue a "fatwa" calling on Iraqi citizens to "take up arms and fight the terrorists and to volunteer and join the forces of security to achieve this sacred purpose" against ISIS.

The Shiite militias responding to the then commander of the IRGC (Islamic Revolutionary Guards Corp) Quds Force, Mayor General Qasem Soleimani, mobilized separately and simultaneously.

Many of the militias responding to Soleimani formed the PMF along with some of the fighters who responded to Sistani's call and remained loyal to him. The militias that responded to Soleimani were and remain close to Iran, and many are U.S.-designated foreign terrorist organizations that killed hundreds of U.S. service members in Iraq between 2003 and 2011.

Since 2016, the PMF has been formalized as an independent entity reporting directly to the Iraqi prime minister, separate from the Iraqi ministries of Defense and Interior.

Some Iraqi officials have described Abu Madi Al Muhandis as a more important representative of Iran than the Iranian embassy itself in Baghdad.

Abu Madi Al Muhandis planned and executed PMF operations while serving as Iran's Iraqi "emissary and messenger."

The Popular Mobilization Committee (PMC), which oversees a range of administrative, planning, and training responsibilities, is formally responsible for ensuring that PMF militias are accountable to the Iraqi federal government.

Fayyadh's installation as chairman of this commission and his relationship with the IRGC (Islamic Revolutionary Guards Corp) protects the PMF from the effective control of the Iraqi federal government, essentially ceding some of what should be the Iraqi government's authority to Tehran.

Most PMF operation commanders are senior members of Iranian-backed militias such as Asaib Ahl al Haq and the Badr Organization. Some simultaneously command a PMF regional operational command and an Iranian-backed individual brigade within the PMF.

PMF regional operational commands plan, conduct, and sustain campaigns and operations within their operational areas.

The PMF's regional operational commands are separate from, but share overlapping areas of responsibility with, the Iraqi Security Forces' regional operational commands. The PMF is not subordinate to the Iraqi Security Forces (ISF) but coordinates many activities with the ISF.

PMF operational commands often collaborate with the ISF to eliminate ISIS remnants.

Iran's co-optation of the PMF command structure down to the operational and tactical levels helps ensure that Iran's representatives and partners in Iraq comply with IRGC guidelines.

However, a small number of PMF brigades are not supported by Iran, but Iranian-backed groups have worked to marginalize and weaken them.

Senior PMF leaders often carry out operations without the approval of the Iraqi prime minister, who is ostensibly the commander in chief of all Iraqi security services.

The PMF and its IRGC "advisers" conducted independent operations during the anti-ISIS campaign, notably near Tikrit in 2015.

Iran-backed Iraqi militias bombed civilians in Tikrit on orders from the IRGC and Iran's proxy Iraqi commanders without the knowledge of the Iraqi government.

The IRGC Quds Force – the IRGC component responsible for covert activities and management of foreign representatives – has also supported ongoing Iraqi militia attacks against US forces in the Middle East, including the attack that killed three US service members in northeast Jordan on June 28, 2024.

IRGC Quds Force commander Esmail Ghaani ordered Iran-backed Iraqi militias to halt attacks on US forces immediately following the June 28, 2024, attack, demonstrating the Quds Force's control over its Iraqi proxies.

Iran's proxy militias in Iraq have also created political wings that grant the militias political cover and allow them to pursue their political and military objectives as quasi-governmental institutions. Militia members supported and helped pass the 2016 PMF Commission Act that institutionalized the PMF.

The political wings also pressure the Iraqi prime minister to pursue policies that further Iranian strategic goals, such as expelling the United States from Iraq.

In January 2020, the Iraqi parliament passed a non-binding resolution to increase pressure on the Iraqi prime minister to order the withdrawal of US forces from Iraq following the US airstrike that killed, for example, Qasem Soleimani and Abu Mahdi al Muhandis.

The Kataib Hezbollah militia threatened to kill the families and staff of lawmakers who opposed the resolution, highlighting the overlap between political and military power in Iraq.

The Badr Organization, another Iranian group, is currently using control of the parliamentary Security and Defense Committee to draft a new resolution to pressure the prime minister to order the withdrawal of US forces from Iraq in response to recent attacks of American self-defense. This was the situation in Iraq in the spring of 2021: chaos!

When meeting the Vatican Gendarmerie operators every evening, they must have wondered what an Italian was doing in the same hotel. Intrigued one evening after dinner, they approached me and asked who I was. I replied that I was a freelancer (aka packaging contractor) and I had been sent by an Italian company that had sold a plant in Baghdad for the packaging of croissants and snacks.

Croissant production line, Al Dalu company (Besmaya Industrial Area, Baghdad)

In reality, I had the feeling that I wasn't believed. However, from that evening on, knowing that I was from Friuli, the bottle of wine was a must.

One day, someone else asked me the same question' "We thought you were a contractor of another type," (the term contractor in English can designate a technician external to a company that provides a service for a fee or even an armed operator with strong military experience who for a fee he fights for a cause; generally they are all expatriates also known as expat).

My past as a former second lieutenant (official forward observer position) at the 185th Parachute Artillery way back in 1985 left its mark over the years.

My military past was quite varied. I CAR (recruit training centre) as an Alpine soldier in Codroipo (UD) and an operational department in Chiusaforte (UD), a charming Carnic village immersed in such a narrow valley where the sun could only be seen for 4 hours a day. They assigned me the 30B (operational situation officer).

They put me in the office next to the battalion commander, a lieutenant colonel, who I asked what I had to do.

He replied, "Haven't you yet understood that your job concerns intelligence?"

"You will be the battalion's spy!"

We will send you together with all the 30B of the Julia brigade to do a month-long course in Merano.

The next day, a jeep took me to the station in Pontebba, and I took the train to Merano.

A lieutenant taught the 30B course, and it was very interesting as it covered topography, survival course, recognition of enemy vehicles (at that time, in the midst of the Cold War, the enemy was the Soviet Union), self-determination of position, patrols, map readings military 1:25,000 and 1:50,000.

One day on leave, I met a very pretty forty-year-old New Zealander of Italian origins who was on holiday in Merano, and I asked her out the following evening. She accepted but told me she would go out with a friend of hers (do they always do this? Who knows why?).

The next day, I went to the lieutenant who was holding the course and asked him if he wanted to go out with me and the two New Zealanders. He replied in the affirmative, and I arranged to meet him in a bar in the center of Merano at 7.00 pm.

I went there a little earlier "on reconnaissance," I met the girl I had met the day before, but she told me that her friend hadn't been able to come, so I waited for the lieutenant, who hadn't arrived yet.

Clearly, he didn't take it well!

I went to dinner with my new friend, and then we spent a few hours in a hotel room, which I paid with the last 20,000 lire (1984) I had left.

I returned to the barracks late at night, around 2.00 am (the entry deadline was 11.00 pm).

The next day, of course, the lieutenant called me to report, and for the rest of my days, I had to stay in the barracks, but it was worth it also because the New Zealander showed up at the hotel with a garter belt that I had never seen in my life, Southern Hemisphere stuff.

After completing the 30B course, I returned to the Chiusaforte barracks and put my heart at rest. I would have had to spend another 9 months in that small Carnic village where there was only a bar and nothingness outside the barracks.

The next day, the incredible happened: the lieutenant colonel commander of the battalion called me to report and told me that he had received a "phone" where it was announced that I had won the competition for reserve officers (I had done the competition in Verona a few months before), and if I wanted, I could go to Bracciano to the artillery school (mountain battery).

During the written test of the competition, there were about seventy of us, and there was a Carabinieri sergeant who went around the desks to make sure that no one was copying the multiple answers of the quizzes from their neighbor. He stopped to talk to me and asked me if I was the son or relative of any army officer. I asked why, and the answer was that I wouldn't have had the slightest chance of entering without knowledge.

I replied that this certainly did not honor the uniform he was wearing, and in the end, he was wrong as I won the competition.

At this point, I had two options:

1. Stay in Chiusaforte for another 9 months in this God-forsaken valley where, in the barracks, many people were starting to go berserk and most likely remain an R.A.S.P.A. = Alpine Recruit Without Any Power. But I would have completed my military service in just 12 months.

2. Go and do the course (5 months) in Bracciano plus another 10 months in the operations department, totaling 18 months with the three months as an Alpine soldier.

I chose the second option because, at least as a second lieutenant, I would have had a salary that would have allowed me to finish my studies in the faculty of electronic engineering (I was missing 5 exams out of 30) without further burdening my parents.

The day before leaving for Bracciano, I was jokingly watering one of my colleagues with a bottle of water in the canteen. The second lieutenant on the picket line immediately noticed me and told me, "Manzan, stay punished."

In the evening, I saw the officer arrive in the dormitory, and he told me that he would "forget" about the punishment if I gave him my "green" suit, which was much newer than his. I told him it was in the laundry and I would give it to him the following day.

The next day, I delivered all the military clothing to the warehouse and said goodbye to the country girl who was leaving the barracks to take me to the Pontebba station. This second lieutenant didn't take it very well either; he will probably still remember it.

They put me in the mountain battery once I arrived in Bracciano at the Artillery School (current headquarters of the 185th Parachute Artillery). I had to start all the training again, starting with the famous "cube."

The school always had two officer-student courses overlapping for 3 months. I was from the 116th course, and I found myself in the 115th course for 3 months as a senior course. We are talking about July 1984. Clearly, the "elders" did their utmost every day to advise the younger students, also known as "pistri" (pistro was the name of the cord that activated the firing pin on howitzers in the past).

The first night, they "stripped" us at 03.00, screaming like crazy, and had us all lined up and covered at attention in our underwear in the corridor.

Some of them had put on the ranks of lieutenant or captain to impress us and give themselves importance. This greatly affected many of us, who were probably sleeping in barracks for the first time and were not used to military life.

For my part, I played along, but in reality, these "elderly people" made me feel a little sorry and a little tender; you could see a kilometer away that it was probably the first time they left home, and they were already frustrated after only 3 months of barracks

We began training with the various commands: attentive, rest, right line, left line, about turn, march in the platoon, and knowledge of the weapon (Garand ca. 7.62 born).

In reality, having already done three months as an Alpine soldier, they were all things that I already knew by heart. Indeed, having attended that wonderful 30B course (operational situation officer, aka intelligence as it is called now), I knew how to read a military map 1:25,000 and 1:50,000. I knew how to self-determine the position by taking the usual 2-3 reference points recognizing Warsaw Pact weapon systems. I had also participated in several night patrols and a basic rock climbing course and was passionate about quickly dismantling and reassembling the Garand.

From a position at attention with the rifle on the ground, it took me 4.5 seconds to disassemble it and 12 seconds to reassemble it.

Clearly, all this annoyed the elders, who began to pick on me. I then considered it absurd that the amphibians had to be shiny and shiny (clean, I would say) because it would not have been logical from a tactical-operational point of view, as they would have been more easily identifiable than an opaque treatment.

This greatly angered the captain who commanded the officer cadet mountain battery. Another absurd thing was to show up in the morning in a platoon in front of the canteen to have breakfast, wait in line for 30 minutes (the artillerymen and senior courses had priority; we officer cadets were nothing), and then arrive when there was only a little watered-down milk left. The croissants (one each) had already clearly been made to disappear by the artillerymen working in the kitchen.

On the other hand, many years later, in Baghdad, I got rid of the desire for croissants by testing a line that produced 600 per minute cases of life! Not to mention, the showers could only be used on Fridays and had water temperatures of 50–55 degrees Celsius without a cold water mixer.

The night guards of the mules (to prevent them from sleeping lying down) in Manziana in the company of a couple of Sardinian claws whose dialect was difficult, if not impossible, to understand represented the height of senseless things. It was all set up to make the students' lives difficult.

And I began to make life more difficult for the senior class by organizing night raids in their dormitory.

At night, two of us would block the elderly man sleeping on the cot with a blanket, and the third would throw pillows at his face.

Clearly, I risked being thrown out of the course several times for disciplinary reasons. Still, I didn't succeed as I was among the first in the written and oral tests, especially in topography and shooting, which are the most important for an artilleryman.

Luckily for me, as deputy battery commander, a paratrooper lieutenant arrived with his amaranth beret from Vannucci (barracks in Livorno, which at the time was home to the 2nd Parachute Battalion, Carabinieri Paratroopers and GIS). He always refused to take off his amaranth beret and put on his Alpine hat.

He took me under his "protection" as I expressed my intention to join the Folgore Brigade once I finished the course.

A month before the end of the course, a parachute captain arrived to recruit for the Folgore Brigade. Five of us responded to the call: I, a Roman (who was confirmed in SPE [effective permanent service] and is now a colonel), a Bolognese who had obtained the TCL (free fall technique) certification as a civilian, and two Tuscans (naturally, to stay closer to home).

After completing the officer cadet course in Bracciano in December 1984, I had 10 days of leave and showed up in Pisa on 2 January 1985 for training for the Military Parachutist licence.

For those who remember, the winter of '84-'85 was one of the coldest after the war until late spring.

It even snowed in Pisa and Livorno, where some houses had no heating.

The training for the certification included various tests, running 5,000 meters in 20 minutes, jumping from the tower, climbing the rope, jumping from 10 m on the round tarp, 5 pull-ups, etc. We did the external tests in half a meter of snow, but we were all enthusiastic and were in our twenties or so.

We were about twenty new second lieutenants from officer cadet schools of infantry, artillery, engineers, and transmissions.

One day, we all went out together from the "Gamerra" barracks, home of the SMIPAR (military parachuting school), now CAPAR (Parachuting Training Centre), to secretly buy the coveted amaranth beret.

Clearly, we did it secretly as we were not yet patented. In the meantime, we were wearing the "stupita," military headgear with a visor. When we returned to the barracks, we found two-second lieutenants wearing Alpino hats in our dormitory!

Maybe you were in the wrong barracks, we told him. The answer was, "We are the Alpine Parachutists," in fact at that time, there was a company of Alpine Parachutists based in Bolzano, which over the years transformed into a Battalion until it transformed a few years ago into the 4th Alpine Parachute Ranger Regiment which on 25 September 2004 moved from Bolzano to Montorio Veronese (VR) subsequently becoming part of the C.O.M.F.O.S.E. (army special forces operations command) operationally dependent on the C.O.F.S. (special forces command).

Certified on 30 January 1985 with the five jumps to obtain the military patent, I was assigned to the 185th Parachute Artillery Group in Livorno. I particularly remember my second commander in the third battery, a captain called:

"Il Perrottone" (famous throughout the Folgore Brigade) was a commander who was always very practical in training.

He was so practical that one day, he gathered us together to teach us how to quickly get off an ACL (light load truck) with a backpack and FAL (light automatic rifle). He organized everything in ten minutes. He put about ten of us in tracksuits who had to simulate the terrorists who would attack the vehicle.

He placed himself on the truck of the ACL, which traveled around the barracks and slowed down near the "terrorists."

Leaning with his left hand on the floor, he jumped off the ACL with his backpack and FAL. He had the misfortune that the wedding ring he was wearing on his ring finger got stuck on a protruding nail. The finger remained on the truck, and he landed on the pavement.

Seeing the scene, a couple of us fainted while he calmly stopped another captain's "five hundred" and asked him if he could take him to the hospital to reattach the finger.

He returned two hours later with his finger reattached and his hand bandaged and had us continue the exercise.

Another event that lingered in my mind was a live fire exercise with our three batteries of 105/14 howitzers at the Monte Romano range. We started with a night exercise during which illuminating flares were fired. The shooting area was delimited by M113s (troop transport vehicles), which were deployed surrounding the shooting area at a safe distance. The truck leader was instructed to stay inside the vehicle with the hatch closed.

A tank master sergeant, probably wanting to see the spectacle of the flares, was left-leaning half-length away; as fate would have it, the bottom of an illuminating rocket (which weighs 10 kg) hit him full-on and literally cut him in two!

Now, the probability of something like this happening is very low but not "zero"; in fact, if we assume the area occupied by the poor sergeant to be 1m square and divide it by the area where the flare cap could have fallen with a radius of around 2km, therefore, A=3.14*4 =12.56 square km i.e. 12,500,000 square m and therefore the probability P=1/12,500,000 i.e. 1 case out of 12.5 million, and yet it happened!

As a second lieutenant, I was a section commander. I had to verify the elevation and direction data of the first three howitzers (six are in the battery). The battery commander (a captain), who acted as a forward observer officer, transmitted the coordinates and altitude of the targets to the firing center (an ACL positioned behind the battery) via radio.

The data began to arrive, and the basic piece (the first howitzer of the battery) adjusted its aim. As soon as the "fork" was made (by fork, we mean a couple of shots fired across the target), the average direction and elevation data for the entire battery were confirmed.

But the elevation reading was one hectograde lower than the previous reading, and I saw all six howitzer barrels lowering frighteningly. I raised the folder saying, "Battery prevented; check again." The lieutenant who commanded the shooting center, probably overcome by the rush of having to shoot quickly at all costs, told me, "Manzan, don't bother me; the aim is correct."

They fired all six howitzers with an incorrect elevation of one hectograde, which at a distance of eight kilometers means firing about 1.5 km shorter. The box of military authorities with various Generals and Colonels was in the firing line, and the shots passed over their heads. Instead of arriving a kilometer and a half from the stage, the first shot arrived a few hundred meters away.

There was a general stampede of "Generals," as they expected the other shots. The lieutenant informed us of the short shot via radio, by the observing officer said to us, "Where the fuck are you shooting?"

I replied, "Where you told us, lieutenant."

Even if to be part of the Vatican Gendarmerie Corps, one must demonstrate an impeccable Catholic faith complete with a letter of introduction from one's parish priest or a prelate, which ensures serious knowledge, even religious, of the person concerned, I am a notary who probably, given that I am from Friuli, they often invited everyone to drink a glass of good wine after dinner. There were also always four gentlemen in dark suits, sunglasses, and earphones in their ears, with good physiques and the usual bulge under the jacket. I thought they would be part of the hotel security.

I asked the Deputy Commissioner with whom I was most familiar, who they were, and he replied that they were from hotel security. I had asked the Italian company I was working for to rent a satellite phone in case of any eventuality. I didn't yet have an Iraqi SIM card in the first few days, but I used it to communicate with Italy.

Whenever I called, these four gentlemen in dark suits looked at me carefully. A satellite phone is easily recognizable as it is much larger than a classic cell phone and has a visible antenna.

After a couple of evenings, seeing that they continued to look at me, I went to them, gave them my business card, speaking in English, and asked them why they were looking at me carefully. One of them took out a card on which the following writing " جهاز المخابرات العراقي " "Jihaz Al-Mukhabarat Al-Amma also called "Mukhabarat," i.e., "Iraqi government intelligence service," to which I didn't ask any further questions, I said goodbye to them and went to sleep. The next morning, Mr. Abu arrived punctually at 07.00 at the reception. He had an ordinary Toyota, which was certainly not armored, with his inseparable M4 resting between him and the door with the muzzle protruding from the window perfectly visible from the outside, always with the safety device inserted and shot in the barrel.

The route we had to travel every day between the Baghdad Hotel and the factory located in the "Besmaya Industrial Area" was about twenty kilometers.

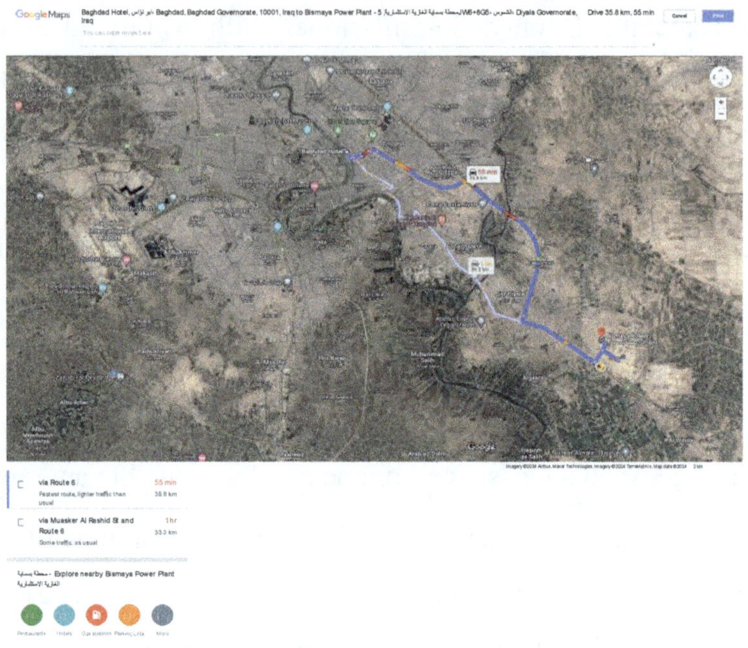

The daily commute from Baghdad Hotel – Factory in Besmaya city

We didn't always take the same route, but sometimes some parts of the route changed. I asked him why. The response was: "I have received information that on that stretch of road, there is a danger of a car bomb attack by ISIS. Nothing but under the ashes!"

About every kilometer, there was an alternating checkpoint: police, army, and militias, all recognizable as the Iraqi police adopt a blue camouflage, the army on sandy brown; let's say the militias are more varied in clothing. The thing that intrigued me was that Mr. Abu, who was escorting me, was the only one who wasn't stopped at the various "checkpoints," but evidently recognizing him, they let us pass through preferential lateral access and even greeted him with a deferential military salute.

Militia Kataib Al Iman Ali in Baghdad

Checkpoint IRAQI POLICE in Baghdad

Checkpoint Iraqi Army

Only once in three weeks of trips to and from the hotel - factory and vice versa, at a checkpoint, a young policeman stopped us, looked inside the car, and, realizing that I was not Iraqi, asked me for my passport, which was clearly in the safety deposit box of the hotel, I had the photocopy with me.

I was about to take out the copy of the passport; Mr. Abu showed his badge to the young policeman, who turned purple, stiffened as if he had seen the devil himself, stood at attention, gave him a military salute, and let us pass, apologizing in a thousand salaams for having stopped us. Mr. Abu winked at me.

I looked at him and asked, "Are you the security manager of the factory, or who are you?"

He replied, "Yes, in fact, I am the security manager of the factory. Each factory is "protected" by a militia, but in reality, I am also a battalion commander of the Kataib Al Iman Ali militia."

Symbol of the Kataib Al Iman Ali militia

Let's say that, militarily speaking, a militia is organized at the level of a large brigade, that is, a few tens of thousands of men. Each militia is, in turn, made up of four to five battalions; therefore, he was at the head of one of these battalions, that is, he commanded a few thousand militiamen, therefore, extremely well known throughout Iraq and beyond.

Now traveling every day escorted by a battalion commander from one of Iraq's most powerful Shiite militias could be an advantage. From a certain point of view, corroborated by the fact that being the head of safety of the factory where I was solving software problems on a line that produced around 150,000 euros of turnover per day, let's say that it had all the advantages of keeping me in good health. In the end, it's all about convenience!

There is a downside that he understood years later.

On February 7, 2024, with the usual procedure with which Qassem Soleimani and Abu Mahdis Al-Muhandis were eliminated, i.e., MQ Reaper-9 drone and Hellfire missile, the Americans carried out a surgical operation in the heart of Baghdad.

The target was an SUV in which three people were traveling, including two leading exponents of Kataib Hezbollah, who are based in Baghdad next to the Military Academy!

In the past, Kataib Hezbollah was one of the Iraqi Shiite militias involved in actions against US targets.

Two of the people killed were Wissam Mohammed "Abu Bakr" al-Saadi and Arkan Al-Aliyawi; the former is considered the "main technical planner of the attacks on American bases in Iraq and Syria." The operation took place in a main artery of the Mashtal neighborhood in the eastern part of the Iraqi capital.

Security forces closed the heavily guarded Green Zone, where numerous diplomatic compounds are located. At the same time, a crowd of protesters chanted anti-American slogans and threatened to march on the US embassy.

The raid occurred "in response to attacks against American service members" and killed "a Kataib Hezbollah commander responsible for planning and directly participating in attacks against American forces in the region," the US military Central Command explained (Centcom), underlining that "there are no indications of collateral damage or civilian casualties."

Before the US claimed responsibility, a security official had reported to AFP (Agence France-Presse) that "a drone launched three rockets at a 4X4 car", targeting "two leaders" of the pro-Tehran group.

A member of the faction had already announced that among those killed was a commander of the group responsible for military affairs in Syria. Earlier, another security official said the struck vehicle was carrying an official from Hashed al-Shaabi, a coalition of mainly pro-Iranian paramilitaries now integrated into Iraq's regular security forces.

I could have been on board that 4x4 SUV three years ago!

07 February 2024 4x4 SUV hit by 3 Hellfire missiles

Funeral of the three Kataib Hezbollah militiamen

Mr. Abu was always very kind towards me. He stopped on the street, and we entered the supermarkets; he invited me to buy what I wanted, such as food and cigarettes, and then he got in line at the cash register to pay (clearly always armed with his M4) and the people recognizing him let him pass.

Never stood in line in three weeks!

One day, he said to me, "Fabiano, but you think that in heaven there is your Christian God and also our Allah; I say that there will only be one, it is evident, because if there were two or more, they would make war even in heaven, what's on the ground is enough."

In fact, the reasoning was logical.

The next day, Mr. Abu asked me if I had ever shot a rifle. I told him yes, but the last time was in 1985 while I was in the military.

If you were able to use a rifle, the situation in Baghdad was still precarious, and you had to be prepared for anything!

I asked if there was a polygon; the polygon was "DIRT BEHIND THE FACTORY." He put a can of Coke 30 meters away and handed me his M4.

Well, he told me, let's see if you remember how to do it; in the factory, every operator who works on the production line and every employee in the office must be.

He emptied almost the entire magazine before grabbing the canister. In the end, I handed him the weapon after removing the magazine and pointing out that there was still a round in the chamber. He didn't flinch, aimed the weapon at the ground about a meter from my feet, and fired the last round in perfect adherence to safety protocols in the style of the Iraqi militia!

One day, he asked me if I had ever heard of another commander of the same militia as him named Ayoub Falih Hasan Al-Rubayie (in Arabic عبّنس الوبيعي who went by the stage name Abu Azrael, literally translated as "**The Father of the Angel of Death.**" He had considered naming his firstborn Azrael after the Angel of Death.

I replied no, and he was greatly surprised; he searched the internet and ultimately understood why.

Abu Azrael is a very famous Kataib Al Iman Ali militia battalion commander, former Taekwondo champion, and fanatic bodybuilder; another nickname was "Iraqi Rambo." He had also created a character on social media, which was followed by millions of followers even outside of Iraq.

They even created an ad hoc cartoon for him where he beats up an ISIS member who was threatening an Iraqi woman by placing himself at his service. He is also a very close friend of Qassem Soleimani.

Abu Azrael and Qassen Soleimani

Abu Azrael with his famous "AXE."

Abu Azrael (alias Iraqi Rambo)

Abu Azrael Cartoon: defending a lady from ISIS

Militians of ISIS

He used to go around with an axe and his famous sword, which he used for a very renowned performance.

First of all, he hated the Americans and, at the same time also, ISIS; his famous motto was:

سن حق ل الٹی ی غبا

(pronounced Hillah Tain) which means, "We will crush you to dust." When he managed to capture a couple of ISIS terrorists alive, he would hang them upside down from a pylon, light a nice fire under their heads, and slowly burn them one at a time so that the others would realize what they were in for shortly thereafter, having finished burning them with his famous sword, he cut them into kebab-style slices.

He posted some videos on this topic on YouTube. Word of his performance reached the ears of Grand Ayatollah Al Sistani, who called him to his presence and reprimanded him by telling him that although it was correct to kill ISIS militants, he shouldn't burn them, cutting them into slices and especially posting these videos online, it wasn't good publicity! For this, he had to repent.

Abu Azrael burning an ISIS militant.

The repentance entailed reciting a couple of prayers while kneeling before Grand Ayatollah Al-Sistani, and consequently, he was granted acquittal!

Abu Azrael was clearly Mr. Abu's close friend because they were both battalion commanders of the same Kataib Al Iman Ali militia

Members of the Kataib Al Iman Ali militia with Mr.Abu and Abu Azrael

Mr. Abu (center) and Abu Azrael (right)

We typically left the hotel around 7:00 a.m. and returned around 6:00 p.m., which roughly aligned with the departures and arrivals of a convoy of about ten armored SUVs. This convoy, escorting the Vatican Gendarmerie, was accompanied by numerous Iraqi service personnel and soldiers. At the front and rear of the convoy were two military vehicles armed with 12 mm machine guns.

Clearly, they did not miss the fact that I was always in the company of Mr. Abu, whom they knew very well.

Sometimes, Mr. Abu called me around 8 pm and told me not to leave the room and to go into the bathtub (which, if made of cast iron, is the safest place in a hotel room).

This happened three or four times, for example, on the night of February 21st. The next day, I read the following news on the internet:

"According to Iraqi military and security sources quoted by the broadcaster 'Rudaw,' at least one rocket hit the headquarters of the National Security Service, which is located near the American Embassy. A note from the Security Media Cell, however, explained that two rockets fell in the Green Zone without causing any casualties."

The episode comes exactly one week after the rocket attack against a base hosting units of the International Anti-ISIS Coalition near Erbil airport, in Iraqi Kurdistan."

Then I understood why I shouldn't leave the room. Rockets were arriving from north to south parallel to my hotel and targeting the Green zone, and I always had the news first! Let's say that the terrace facing west gave me a preferential view of these attacks.

Preferential west side view from the Baghdad Hotel on the Tigris River and "Green Zone."

The following day I asked Mr. Abu if it was ISIS who fired the rockets; he slyly looked at me, smiling and shaking his head, and told me: "It's our militias; the Americans haven't yet understood that they have to leave, they try to impose their model of democracy with the sound of bombs, here in Iraq it doesn't work like that, we defend ourselves against the invasion... if some foreign nation overran your country to impose their model of democracy you would be happy?"

He wasn't entirely wrong!

The Islamic State, he told me, "is an invention of the Americans in cahoots with Saudi Arabia."

"ISIS came from the north to the gates of Baghdad, occupied the oil wells and killed those who worked there, then extracted the oil and resold it to Turkey, transporting it with tank trucks to the Turkish border; we have the evidence!" and I thought: but Turkey is part of NATO, an increasingly complicated situation.

I asked him a very delicate question, given that the US-led international coalition also includes Italians, whether he considered a difference in behavior between Americans and Italians towards the Iraqis.

The answer was: "Italians spread culture and military assistance, while Americans spread blood and devastation."

He had good memories, especially of our "Special Forces" with regard to "military assistance."

He seemed sincere in his answer, or perhaps he wanted to give me a political answer. I will probably never know.

I thought Turkey, which is part of NATO and, among other things, continues to bomb the Iraqi Kurds on the Turkey-Iraq border, and we Italians, with our special forces, have trained the armed wing of the Iraqi Kurds, i.e., the Peshmerga to fight against ISIS.

Not to forget the battles of the 3 bridges of Nassiriya, which includes various episodes that occurred a few months after the attack on 12 November 2003 at the Maestrale base; from 6 April to 6 August 2004, several battles took place between the Italian troops and the Army of Mahdi (another Shiite militia in competition with that of Kataib Hezbollah).

The Italian soldiers were engaged in several clashes in the city, in which over 30,000 bullets were fired, to control three bridges that allowed crossings over the Euphrates river; eleven Bersaglieri were slightly injured, while Iraqi losses were heavier (around 200 victims, and the same number wounded). It appears that a woman and two children among the civilians died. There's no denying it's real chaos, with everyone against everyone.

On the evening of February 2, while I was at the bar drinking a beer in the company of an Iraqi who used to drink a bottle of whiskey in a couple of hours, three of the Iraqi services approached me and tapped me on the shoulder.

I turned around, and they said, "Mr. Manzan, you have 15 minutes to prepare your luggage; we have to transfer you to another hotel for security reasons."

I asked if I could check it out the following day, but they firmly refused.

I went to my room, packed my suitcase, and called my former commander in Italy when I was at the 185th parachute artillery. I explained the situation to him.

He didn't answer immediately; there was a pause for 5 seconds (knowing him, usually when I call him, he interrupts me and doesn't even let me finish the first sentence, but in this case, he understood that the situation was really critical and thought about it) finally he said to me "Fabiano, do exactly what they say" and touch your balls while I make a few phone calls.

I also called Mr. Abu to explain the situation. He was so enraged that he spoke to me for five minutes in Arabic; he then realized I didn't understand; switching to English, he told me they had no right to move me to another hotel. It was a very complicated situation.

I told him I would call him when I got to the Palestine Hotel, and so I did; he calmed down. Those three gentlemen with sunglasses and earphones were waiting for me in the hotel lobby, settling the open accounts at the cash register themselves, and they gave me the receipt for what Mr. Abu had already paid. I would say the height of honesty!

I got into the car with them, hoping that it was a hotel transfer and not a trip to another destination, perhaps to one of their offices with related interrogation; poor Giulio Regeni came to mind.

In fact, we arrived at the Palestine Hotel I had visited a few weeks before, and I noticed it was still empty. It was better than nothing, I thought.

Clearly, I couldn't sleep; there were several thoughts in my head; maybe they would come to pick me up because they thought it strange that I was staying in the same hotel as the Vatican Gendarmerie, escorted by a militia commander.

At 03.00, I received a WhatsApp message from an Iraqi number that I didn't have in my address book, which said:

"Good evening, Mr. Fabiano, a message from the Italian Embassy here in Baghdad...

We have heard about some misunderstanding at the Baghdad hotel... can we talk about it?"

I readily agreed and scheduled a meeting at the Palestine Hotel for the following evening.

In the evening, two individuals arrived; one had a lean, athletic physique, while the other seemed to me to be a bespectacled office employee. At the factory that same day, I asked for a box of croissants and placed it next to the table where we sat.

I asked if they wanted to have a coffee, and they replied in the affirmative, perhaps also with something to eat. I told him that to accompany the coffee, I brought you a whole box of freshly baked croissants from the production line today, which is clear proof that I was there on business!

But since they were hesitant, I ate one first and let them choose.

Who knows what they were thinking? I handed him my business card and said, "I guess you don't have yours with you." I was right!

Surely, the one with the athletic physique was an ex-military man, most likely ex-special forces; I was sensing it from his very determined way of speaking, from his watch, and from how he looked around with his eyes without moving his head.

They told me: "Mr. Fabiano, you have missed two crucial things. Even though you registered your trip on the Ministry of Foreign Affairs website and provided your flight details, you should have also communicated the hotel where you would be staying, the address of the factory where you would work, and your daily commute. Additionally, upon arriving at Baghdad airport, you needed to call the Italian Embassy immediately to confirm your arrival. In Baghdad, dozens of Italians arrive daily; we cannot run after everyone."

He continued, "The second bullshit was being escorted by Mr. Abu, who, as you will have understood, being a battalion commander of the Kataib Al Iman Ali militia, is well known throughout Iraq. Militias such as Kataib Al Iman Ali, Kataib Hezbollah, and other militias act in parallel with the Iraqi government but try not to step on each other's toes, but the situation is very confusing; there is no black and white here the different tones of gray are all 'agenda.'"

I replied that the escort company could not operate as Baghdad was under curfew due to Covid (this was what they had told me, or perhaps they wanted to save the 1,200 euros per day). Mr. Abu was the only solution the factory owner had found.

They shook their heads, "In fact, when Italian SMEs (small and medium-sized companies) sell machinery in these parts, they don't worry about organizing the safety of the technicians. They delegate everything to the end customer to save money, and then these things happen. To save money, the Iraqi client did not call a private close protection company that could still operate even in the Covid era. Last night, the Iraqi services called us and asked us if we knew you and if we were aware that you were in Baghdad. We did our research and understood that you were clean, but be very careful about associating with certain people. I thanked them for the advice and went to my room."

The technical manager of the factory line was a very smart engineer named Mister M., about 35 years old, who I asked for information regarding the situation in Baghdad, which seemed very chaotic to me.

He had worked in the oil fields for several years and sometimes had to remove the disturbance very quickly because the next day, ISIS arrived to take possession. He gave me a lot of useful advice and informed me that many factory employees were supporters of various militias, so be careful how you speak!

One day, I noticed that I had heard rumors that the news had spread in the factory that I would have fought in the famous second battle of Mosul, where ISIS had been defeated.

I had all the production line staff gather together during the break and explained that this was utterly false. I reported to Mister

M. in English, and he translated it into Arabic. The translation seemed to be correct, as several people came to apologize.

One day, Mister M. told me a story that seemed taken from a spy story novel by "Gerald de Villiers," a well-known crime author with his protagonist CIA agent out of character "Malko Linge."

I did further checks on this story from other sources, and it turned out to be true. What he told me was the following:

Saddam Hussein, who took power as President of Iraq in 1979, immediately carried out a purge, sentencing several political opponents to death and accusing them of high treason; so far, everything was normal. He completed work on a new Ministry of Finance building in Baghdad.

Having learned of the project, the Mossad (Israel's external secret service) managed to infiltrate a couple of "trusted designers" into the English construction company. At the end of construction, the two designers "affiliated" with the Mossad and proposed surrounding the building with a pedestrian walkway (or something similar) in a triangle.

Once finished, they designed and had another 180° built but canceled the first triangle from the project.

It was impossible to understand at ground level given the size of the two triangles, the perimeter of which was several hundred meters, and the formation of a "Star of David" symbol of the flag of Israel.

Saddam Hussein, who in the meantime was commemorating the "pseudo victory" over Iran after eight years of war, received a telex in his office from the Mossad saying that the largest Star of David in the world had been placed in the center of Baghdad.

Evidently, Saddam Hussein, who was on bad terms with Israel, unleashed his officials for months to find out where this Star of David could be, which could be a flag or a painting on a building, but they found nothing. After a few months, they sent him a satellite photo showing the scam.

Ministry of Finance in Baghdad

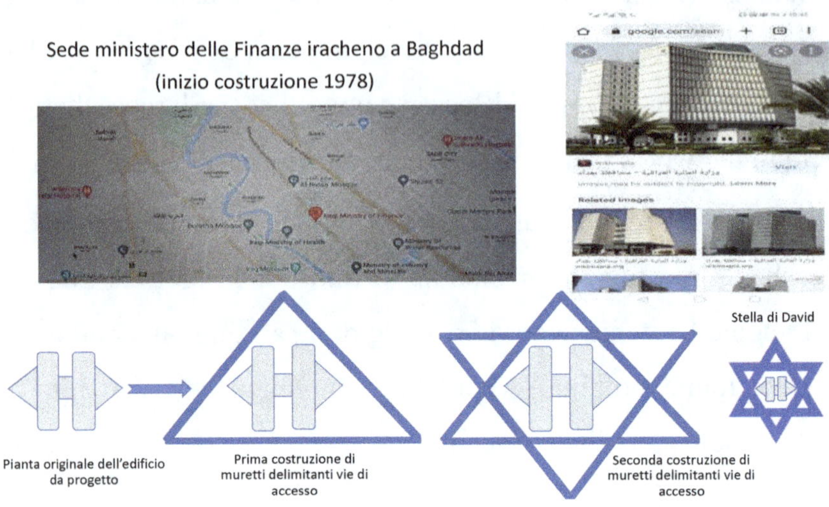

أكبر نجمة اسرائيلية في العالم تقع في بغـداد ! (فيـديو حصري)

The reaction of Saddam Hussein, who was no stranger to purges, was as follows: he had all the designers who had worked on the project hanged along a bridge except the two Mossad agents, who had clearly disappeared in the meantime.

I would say classic **SIGINT** (signal intelligence) and **HUMINT** (human intelligence) operations by the Mossad. Upon my return to Italy, the territorial commander of the Carabinieri called me to the barracks. He asked me what I was doing in Baghdad; I told him I was there for work.

How did he know I was in Baghdad?

The following events occurred:

The Iraqi services called the Italian Embassy, which, in turn, was called the AISE (Italian External Security Agency) in Rome.

AISE called the regional command of the Carabinieri in Udine, CC Company for territorial jurisdiction, and going down the level, the request for information reached the territorial command of the Carabinieri, where I am a resident. Luckily, the territorial commander knew me very well, so I could imagine the answer.

Let's say a series of phone calls that will have worried various people.

18 UDINE

RICCARDO DE TOMA

LA STORIA

L'ingegnere friulano che scommette sul futuro dell'Iraq «Anche se pericoloso»

Article in the newspaper "Messaggero Veneto"

Were there any consequences? I would say yes. A few months after my return, having to go to the United States, I connected to the US embassy website to obtain the ESTA (Electronic system for travel authorization). It is a very simple procedure to obtain a tourist visa. You fill out an online form asking for some information and pay around 80 USD.

In the form, you must answer the following questions:

• General information

• Copy of passport valid for at least 6 months from the time of arrival in the United States

• If you have worked for intelligence agencies

• If you served in the military, where and with what rank

• You have been to one of these 5 countries: Iran, Iraq, Syria, Yemen, and North Korea.

Of course, the worst thing you can do to an American public official (embassy official) is to lie, so I replied that I had been to Iraq. At this point, the procedure was interrupted; it was no longer possible to have the ESTA online, but you had to make an appointment at the Embassy or Consulate through one of their agencies and produce a whole further series of documentation, for example, a document justifying why I had been in Iraq, a letter from my bank stating "Financial Capacity," educational qualification, military discharge certificate, etc...

Let's say that the "Appreciation Letter" that the factory owner in Baghdad gave me at the end of the work had its effect!

NO : 786

Baghdad , 3rd of March , 21

Letter of Appreciation

We ALDALU Company extend our sincere appreciation to the exerted efforts presented by Mr. Fabiano Manzan as he did very good job to maintain and inspect our lines performance on regular basis during his availability.

* Copy of this letter to ALDALU Archive .

Yours Faith Fully ,

Adnan J. Jarallah

CEO of ALDALU Company

Iraq-Baghdad-Russifa –Near Bismayah city project
Mobile: 00962799807908/009647704429422/009647801984996
E-mail:- adnan@alhadara-group.com
Website: www.alhadara-group.com

CHAPTER 3: THE "SACRISTAN" BOLD INCURSION

A.I. Sgt. Monte Odino 8th Arditi Incursori Caimani Course 1957

I have always had a passion for the various Special Forces departments. We in Italy have various international excellence, including the GOI (Gruppo Operativo Incursori) department of the Navy. I remember a few years ago, I was near Parma for work and staying in a hotel. Coming back in the evening, I found some pick-ups and vans with the license plate "MM" (Navy) in the parking lot; I asked myself: what is the Navy doing on the hills of Parma?

The next morning, I found myself having breakfast with the entire 3rd "HAUNGRY" Platoon of the GOI in a vegetative state with a beautiful "patch" with the symbol of the X-MAS and a "hungry" crocodile.

At dinner, I offered them a bottle of wine and complimented them on what they had done and still do. While I was organizing an event entitled "**DALLA SCUOLA DI SDRICCA A QUELLA DEL SERCHIO, GLI ARDITI ITALIANI INTERRA E IN MARE**" for 8 November 2024 in Aquileia (Ud) in collaboration with **ANMI** (National Association of Italian Sailors) of Gemona with the participation of the C.V. Vittorio Russo, former commander of the operational group of raiders (GOI), natural heirs of the Xth MAS Flotilla, I remembered that someone told me that the oldest Ardito Incursore of the Navy still alive lived in San Giorgio di Nogaro.

I inquired and discovered that he was the uncle of a friend of mine; I asked to go and see him and if he wanted to be invited to the event that would be held in Aquileia with the patronage of the Municipality itself, rejected by the Municipality of San Giorgio di Nogaro...who knows why?

It was a very hot afternoon in June 2024. I went to his house (he lived 200 meters from my house), I rang the doorbell and his wife came to open the door for me and said to me, "Good evening engineer, my husband is waiting for you at home, given the outside temperature of 40 degrees with 80% humidity it is not appropriate to let it out." I entered and found myself in front of a little man of around 70kg, 170cm tall, in perfect physical shape that would make a twenty-year-old envious; he could have been around 80 years old (in reality, he was 89), lively eyes who were always looking around, a very kind way of speaking, but extremely decisive.

I looked at him with amazement and said to him, "But you are the sacristan of our parish; I see you in the church while you come to collect the offerings, and you are always in the front row carrying the cross in the procession of Our Lady of Sorrows in the village."

He replied in the affirmative; in fact, people knew him as **"THE SACRISTAN."** Did anyone know that he had spent a lifetime in the Persian Gulf as a diver for various oil and gas companies?

In reality, few people knew that he was a navy raider of the 8th Caimani course way back in 1957, a year in which officially our special forces still could not hesitate given the "Treaties of Paris" in 1947, which prevented the reconstitution of special forces and means of assault in the Navy. The Allies were evidently mindful of the damage the 10th Mas flotilla had caused the English during the Second World War.

His name is ODIN MONTE, and he was a Marine Raiders sergeant, the grandfather of the current GOI (Raider Operational Group).

I told him, "But now I remember you when I was 10-12 years old, and I came to steal your cherries from your famous tree in the courtyard. I tried to run away, but you, who was about 40 years old at that time, always caught me because you were much quicker than me." He began to show me his memory album with all the photos of the various courses before the 8th course.

All were deceased in operation, training, or old age, and his face moved. He told me various episodes, two of which stuck in my mind. The first concerned the famous Palmaria swimming tour.

Palmaria is an island located in front of Varignano Bay, the current headquarters of the Navy Raiders, and since the 1st Raider course (1952), it was one of the barring tests (if you failed, you were expelled from the course).

The test consisted of circumnavigating the island, which is approximately 7/8 km long, half in favor and half against the current. You must pass the test equipped only with a mask and fins in a maximum of 2 hours and 30 minutes. You could also bring a canteen of water, but he and a friend of his from Padua thought it best, as good Friulians and Venetians, to fill it with a good Merlot to give themselves courage.

In the end, they passed the test, but they reached the finish line with, let's say, an alcohol level closer to 2 mg/liter than 1 mg/liter... drunk, to say the least, and were put in prison for three days (CPR) with relative "bullshit," incidentally to those who are not accustomed to military terms, the term "cazziatone" indicates a verbal and unwritten reprimand, consequently nothing remains on the characteristic notes.

Things from other times!

There are rumors that some raider students during this test in those days filled their water bottles with minestrone mixed with wine! Hunger reigned at all hours, day and night. Then he told me another of his crazy exploits. One day, he left the Varignano barracks on free leave; in those days, wearing the white uniform in the summer (with white chalk in the pocket to cover any stains) was mandatory. Still with his friend from Padua, they returned to the hotel at 3.00 am and found the door closed. They had just finished the rock climbing course a few days ago (of which he later went on as an instructor). They took advantage of the experience of the course, climbed along the eaves, and entered the first open window on the third floor.

There, they found themselves in the bedroom of two newlyweds on their honeymoon who were copulating under the sheets and looked at the two sailors in horror.

The two raiding students stood at attention, saluted, and introduced themselves as members of the Navy with their name and rank. They immediately left from the door that led to the corridor, apologizing as they made their way through the door.

The following day, the newlyweds packed their bags hurriedly, not even having breakfast.

It seems that they never returned to that hotel!

CHAPTER 4: ADDIS ABEBA (Ethiopia)

On one of my business trips, I ended up in Addis Ababa, the capital of Ethiopia, in February 2019, a non-leap year (as we know, leap years occur every 4 years.)

What immediately struck me about this former Italian colony was the availability and friendship of the local population when they realized that you were Italian. In the factory, all mechanical terms were Italian, from hammer, gauge, wrench, etc… clearly an obvious consequence of our colonization.

On February 28th, the factory manager called me to the office and told me that the following day, March 1st, the factory would be closed in observance of Ethiopia's national holiday.

My curiosity immediately forced me to search the internet to understand which event the national holiday was being observed. The following day, March 1, they would commemorate the famous battle of Adua where our Gen. Oreste Baratieri, in command of around 20,000 soldiers, thought he was facing 30,000-40,000 locals armed with bows and arrows, but in reality, he had received completely incorrect information from our "services" and found himself facing an army of 120,000 soldiers, 80,000 of whom were armed with firearms.

The war began in December 1895, when Ethiopian troops attacked the scattered Italian garrisons in the Tigray region, which had been occupied the previous April; the Italians had been taken by surprise and immediately suffered defeat in the battle of Amba

Alagi on December 7. Added to this defeat was the surrender of the Macallè garrison on 22 January 1896, which had resisted a siege that lasted two months.

The Italian forces under the command of General Oreste Baratieri, now reinforced by fresh troops arriving from Italy, massed in the area between Adigrat and Edagà Amus, but Menelik's army bypassed the enemy deployment and headed towards the Adua area, thus finding itself in an excellent position to attempt the invasion of the Italian colony of Eritrea. Baratieri tried to parry this move by changing the front of his deployment from south to west, moving his troops to the Enticcius region and settling on a solid defensive position on Mount Saatì on 7 February, just a few kilometers from the Ethiopian camp located in the valley of Adua.

The two armies faced each other for the next twenty days and remained in their respective positions. The negus took advantage of this inactivity to start diplomatic negotiations, even going so far as to offer the cessation of hostilities in exchange for the abrogation of the Uccialli treaty, whose controversial clauses were one of the causes of the war; this request, however, was rejected by the Italian government, now convinced that only full military success would allow Italian prestige in the region to be re-established. Concerned about Baratieri's inactivity, Prime Minister Francesco Crispi began to encourage the general to achieve a decisive victory as soon as possible, sending him a famous telegram on 25 February:

«This is a military consumption, not a war; small skirmishes in which we always find ourselves outnumbered by the enemy; unsuccessful waste of heroism. I have no advice to give because I'm not on site, but I note that the campaign is without a preconception, and I would like it to be established. We are ready to make any sacrifice to save the honor of the army and the prestige of the Monarchy. »

On the evening between 28 and 29 February, Baratieri gathered his collaborators again to inform them of his decisions: the Italian army would not directly attack the Ethiopian positions, considered too strong, but would advance under cover of night to occupy a series of hills closer to the enemy deployment; in this way, Baratieri would have forced Menelik either to accept the fight by attacking the Italian troops deployed in a more favorable position or to give up the field and retreat. The troops of the Italian Expeditionary Force were then divided into four brigades, entrusted to the four generals: Dabormida would lead the right wing, with the task of settling on the hill of Rebbì Ariennì, Albertone would lead the left wing, tasked with occupying the hill Chidanè Merèt, Arimondi would have held the center, partially standing on the same hill Rebbì Ariennì in a slightly further back position, while Ellena would have led the reserve, deployed behind Arimondi. In Baratieri's intentions, the various brigades would be able to guarantee mutual support, wiping out any enemy attack with crossfire.

The Italians fielded 550 officers, 10,550 national soldiers, and 6,700 indigenous soldiers (the àscari), which comprised 17,800 men with 56 artillery pieces. Apart from a few "chosen" troops (such as the Bersaglieri and the Alpini, the majority of the Italian units were made up of conscripts, drawn from their regiments in Italy to serve in Africa (when they were not sent there as punishment); composed of men of various origins, the units almost totally lacked esprit de corps or war experience, as well as adequate training for the environment in which they found themselves operating. The equipment was of low quality, especially regarding shoes. While the Italian units, for reasons of uniformity of ammunition with the indigenous units, had been re-equipped with the Vetterli-Vitali Mod. 1870/87 rifle, which was more advanced than the Carcano Mod. 91 with which the units had trained at home askari were of discontinuous value: the units recruited in Eritrea were considered the best, while those from Tigray, a recently occupied region, were considered unreliable.

Although the Adua region had been under Italian occupation since April 1895, Baratieri did not have a reliable map of the area; instead, the brigade commanders were provided with a freehand sketch of the positions to be occupied—an imprecise and highly inaccurate depiction. The lack of cavalry units made preliminary reconnaissance of the battlefield impossible.

According to the information received, Baratieri estimated the strength of the Ethiopian army at between 30,000 and 40,000 men, demoralized by disease and food shortages; Menelik's troops, on the other hand, numbered between 100,000 and 120,000 men, of which around 80,000 were equipped with some type of firearm.

The result was a resounding defeat, and from there began the end of our colonization in the Horn of Africa.

I thought it would be appropriate not to leave the hotel the next day as it could happen that some nostalgic local, knowing that I was Italian, would have an "unfriendly" attitude.

Towards the evening, I received a phone call from the factory manager, and he told me, "Tomorrow, be at the reception at 09.00, and I will pick you up."

I arrived punctually, and we went to a couple of commemorations for the national holiday. He introduced me to various civil and military authorities as an Italian technician who was testing a snack production line in his factory.

Seeing that I was embarrassed, he took me aside and said:

"The Ethiopian people are very friends with the Italian people; it is true that during your colonization, you killed tens of thousands of people, but what was much more important is that you left us your way of working, your craftsmanship, and your imagination." Not to mention the Italian art of love that great-great-grandmothers, great-grandmothers, and grandmothers have handed down from generation to generation up to the present day; in fact, during the colonization of this area of the Horn of Africa, we built 5,000 km of roads. The state roads of Italian East Africa are the major communication road infrastructures included in the transport plan of the 'Azienda Autonoma Strade Statali (AASS),' which from 1936 to 1941 was built by fascist Italy in the territories of Italian East Africa (AOI). Among these, the famous Via Imperial stands out, which connects Addis Ababa with Mogadishu (about 1400 KM). Also the longest freight transport cableway in the world. It was built in16 months of work and had a total length of 75.05 km (of which 71.8 of the direct Massawa-Asmara line, plus 3.2 km for the Zaga-Moncullo branch); at the time of construction, it was the longest tribune system of the world. It is considered an authentic engineering marvel of the time since the daily transport capacity (in 10 hours of operation) was equal to that of four trains (about 400 tons of goods).

Construction began in 1935 and was completed in March 1937 but was closed a few years later, in 1941, due to damage from the Second World War. It was dismantled by the British in 1951 and brought to their home.

The cableway started from Massawa, located on the Red Sea, with two sections (one from the Champ de Mars and the other from the ammunition depot) that converged in Zaga. The connection continued in subsequent nine sections, passing through Dogali, Mai Atal, Sabarguma, Ghinda, and Nefasit, finally reaching the terminus of Godaif, the southern district of Asmara, at an altitude of 2,326 meters above sea level. The route crossed over 70 kilometers, crossing the mountains and valleys that separated the two terminal cities: from Asmara to Nefasit, the route was straight, while from Nefasit to the sea, it was slightly curved. Due to the longitudinal extension and the large difference in height between the sea and the Asmara plateau, the cableway crossed all the climatic and meteorological situations of the country (from the sea heat, it was easy to encounter rain and wind, and then finally find the cool high mountains). For this reason, the tipper wagons were equipped with a waterproof cover.

CHAPTER 5: ŞANLIURFA (TURKEY)

In April 2024, I was commissioning in the Şanlıurfa area of the ancient "Cappadocia," 55 km from the border with Syria.

The final customer (end-user) is one of the most essential Turkish pharmaceutical companies, Dollvet, and a producer of vaccines, including the "TURCOVAC" against Covid-19.

Urfa, officially called Şanlıurfa (Turkish pronunciation: [ʃanˈɫɯɯɾfa]), is a city in southeastern Turkey and the capital of Şanlıurfa Province. The city was known as Edessa from the Hellenistic era until the Christian era. Urfa is located on a plain about 80 km east of the Euphrates. Its climate is characterized by sweltering, dry summers and cool, humid winters.

About 12 km northeast of the city is the famous Neolithic site of Göbekli Tepe, the oldest known temple in the world, founded in the 10th millennium BC. The area was part of a network of early human settlements where the agricultural revolution occurred.

Because of its association with Jewish, Christian, and Islamic history and the legend that it was the birthplace of Abraham, Urfa is nicknamed the "City of the Prophets."

Religion is important in Urfa. The city "has become a center of fundamentalist Islamic beliefs" and is considered one of the most "devoutly religious cities in Turkey."

The city is located 30 miles from the Atatürk Dam, in the heart of the Southeast Anatolia project, which draws thousands of rural villagers to the city each year in search of work.

On this trip, the team was made up of the writer, two Turkish technicians, a mechanic, and an electrician.

The programmer who developed the software in Italy for this machine to fill bottles of the "Turcovac" vaccine, as soon as he realized that he would have to go and test the machine in Turkey, 55 km from the border with Syria, he probably gave up because in this area the "Kurdistan Worker's Party," i.e., the PKK is still active. In reality, the most dangerous Turkish border area is currently on the border with Iraq.

However, the "lodging" was exceptional at the Double Tree by Hilton; the only flaw is that in this area of Turkey, not even the reception of a Hilton speaks English.

In these cases, getting organized with voice translator software on your phone is the least you need to do. We are in the month of Ramadan, so those who observe it must not eat, drink, or smoke from sunrise to sunset; after sunset, one is free to eat and drink.

The curious thing was that both Turkish technicians were of Islamic religion, only that the electrician was a profound observant of Ramadam; therefore, with a temperature of 40 degrees, do not drink from sunrise to sunset, the result was that at 2 in the afternoon, he had to stay seated to avoid fainting.

The mechanic ate and drank usually; indeed, in the evening, beer and wine were always on the table. Türkiye, a country where the West meets the East!

Sometimes, it happened to see a group of girls enter the hotel restaurant, some wearing the "burka," some with the veil, and some in a miniskirt, all friends with each other. It was fantastic to see how everyone respected everyone in this place.

The first week, the President of Turkey, Erdogan, arrived to support the current governor of Şanlıurfa Salih Ayhan during the local elections campaign.

The hotel was filled with about a hundred security personnel for President Erdogan, which made me feel "very protected."

The second week, the Governor of Şanlıurfa organized a dinner with 400 people in the hotel, and at the end, everyone lined up to shake his hand, a 2-hour procession!

I called one of the two Turkish colleagues. I told him to go to the governor's head of security and inform him that we were an "Italian-Turkish team" who was testing a machine produced in Italy in the Dollvet factory. Maintaining strong commercial-political relations is good for everyone. Italy is always well-regarded and admired abroad for its creativity, craftsmanship, and imagination!

The Governor of Şanlıurfa Salih Ayhan.

Once the procession of greetings to the guests was over, the head of security whispered something in the ear of the governor, who looked at me and came towards me, who was "coincidentally" at the reception.

He greeted me, shaking my hand warmly (he spoke a little in Italian and a little in English) and complimenting me. I was told that we would see each other at the factory the next day since he had already planned the visit to Dollvet.

In a Dollvet-style "white atmosphere" operational suit

On March 29th, while I was taking the connection to Venice in Istanbul after having tested this vaccine production line at Dollvet and having tried in my own small way to foster commercial relations. Italian-Turks, Mrs. Anna Camposampiero, coming on a flight from Italy, was blocked at the airport in Istanbul.

I quote the article from the 'Giornale Comunista online Contropiano precisely:'

«Our comrade Anna Camposampiero, of the national secretariat of Rifondazione and of the executive of the European Left, candidate for the European elections in the "Peace, Land, Dignity" list, has currently been blocked at Istanbul airport.»

Maurizio Acerbo, national secretary of the Communist Refoundation Party, denounced the affair involving the activist and exponent of the Milanese left, which reports some of the messages that Camposampiero has sent in the last few hours directly from Istanbul.

«They stopped me, locked me in a room, took a mug shot, and confiscated my passport. I'm waiting to find out which flight I'll be repatriated on." For Acerbo, «his expulsion is an unacceptable act by a country which, let us remember, is part of NATO and is therefore officially an ally of Italy.»

From Rifondazione, they recall that Anna Camposampiero has always been involved in international issues, from Latin America to Kurdistan.

She is particularly active in solidarity with the Kurdish people and the democratic and feminist movements in Turkey and had to play the role of the observer in the elections at the invitation of the Green Left party born after the outlawing of the "Hdp party" and has been "several times in Turkey as an observer, with international delegations for the defense of human rights, to participate in congresses of the Kurdish left."

«In Erdogan's Turkey – concludes Acerbo – the repression continues to affect the opposition forces, the left-wing movements, and in particular the Kurdish one.»

In the late afternoon of Friday, 29 March, Camposampiero also denounced the incident with a post on Facebook: *«I left for Turkey this morning invited by my Kurdish comrades for the local elections on Sunday 31 March. I had to carry out my role as an observer in the elections at the invitation of the Green Left party, born after the outlawing of the HDP party, but in Erdogan's Turkey, the repression continues to affect opposition forces, left-wing movements and in particular the Kurdish one ».*

But *«when I arrived in Istanbul at 5 pm local time, I was stopped at passport control and taken to a room. They took my passport and luggage, fingerprints, and mug shot. I refused to sign a document whose contents I did not understand, and I refused to hand over my cell phone. I am locked in a room with four other people awaiting expulsion.»*

At this point, "the woman allegedly asked to speak to the Italian Consulate, and I was told that I could contact the Turkish Consulate upon my return. There is an Armenian girl whose cell phone was taken away who had a panic attack and burst into tears. I don't know how long I'll be here. There is no cultural mediator, and no one speaks English. And above all, no one tells you anything. After years of fighting administrative detention, I am experiencing it firsthand."

On Saturday morning, Maurizio Acerbo, national secretary of Rifondazione Comunista, announced that *«Anna Camposampiero was expelled from Turkey and put on a flight to Italy. It should arrive at Bergamo airport at 11.»*

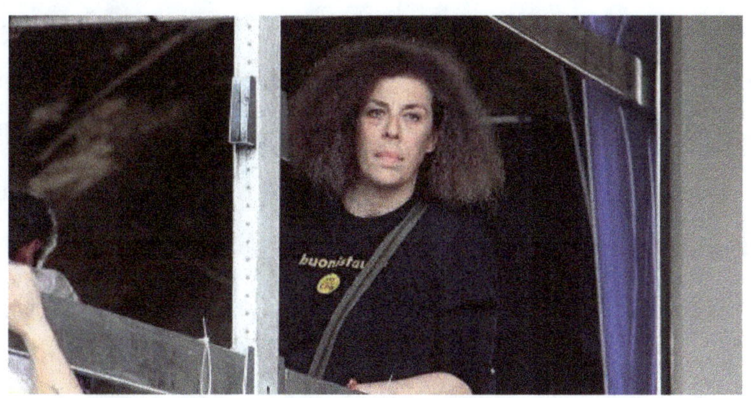

Anna Camposampiero, activist of "Rifondazione Comunista" and of the executive of the European Left

CONCLUSION:

Different approaches, different results…

I would recommend to Mrs. Anna Camposampiero a complete immersion in a travel risk course focused on the topic "Awareness," which I will talk about in the next chapter.

CHAPTER 6: ANALYTICAL SUMMARIES (TRAVEL RISK)

In this last chapter, I will try to analyze the travel risks faced by a traveler, i.e., a technician or salesperson, but also by a doctoral student from a university who goes abroad or a simple tourist.

I will try to simplify as much as possible the various theoretical procedures learned at the "Travel Risk" course organized by Polis Open Learning by combining them with my practical experience in the field.

I will also make a summary of the laws currently in force in Italy regarding the regulations currently in force. I will try to analyze the mistakes I made and my Italian clients committed at the time, especially in Baghdad, linking them to what I subsequently learned by certifying myself as

"SECURITY MANAGER ISO/UNI 10459" and awaiting SECURITY TRAVEL UNI/PDR 124/22 update certification. 12.09.2023

Let's start by saying any "client" company that gives an assignment to a technician (or salesman) who goes abroad, who we will call a "traveler," to carry out the commissioning of any system or for a sales negotiation with the customer called "end user" must be protected against all risks.

This concept is also valid for universities that have doctoral students abroad.

The three stakeholders, therefore, are:

• CLIENT

• THE TRANSFER TRAVELER

• END-USER

Evidently, the traveler during the trip is subject to an "endogenous" risk (within the company where he will work) but also to an "exogenous" risk, i.e., external to the company.

A mathematical formula gives the term "risk" in this case:

R=P*I, where "R" is the risk, "P" is the probability that a harmful event will occur, and "I" is the impact, which can be pecuniary, physical, psychological, image-related, etc…

The PROBABILITY "P" is divided into 5 classes:

1-Low probability

2-Probability attention

3-High probability

4-High probability

5-Critical probability

IMPACT "I" is also divided into 5 classes

1-Not significant

2-Minimum

3-Medium

4-High

5-Catastrophic

Through a risk assessment using a risk validation document (DVR) drawn up by a subject expert, if the product R=P*I

R<=1 Low (No impact)

2<= R <=3. Manage and monitor risk with normal operational management activities

4<= R <=9 Risks must be managed and monitored to reduce them to the lowest level reasonably possible (ALARP)

10<= R <=19 Significant risk management to reduce it to the minimum reasonably possible (ALARP)

20<= R <=25 Immediate risk management. Do not proceed and inform senior management.

<table>
<tr><td rowspan="3">Probabilità</td><td colspan="8" style="text-align:center">Impatto</td></tr>
<tr><td></td><td></td><td>1</td><td>2</td><td>3</td><td>4</td><td>5</td></tr>
<tr><td></td><td></td><td>Non Significativo</td><td>Minimo</td><td>Medio</td><td>Alto</td><td>Catastrofico</td></tr>
<tr><td>CRITICO</td><td>5</td><td>5</td><td>10</td><td>15</td><td>20</td><td>25</td></tr>
<tr><td>ALTO</td><td>4</td><td>4</td><td>8</td><td>12</td><td>16</td><td>25</td></tr>
<tr><td>ELEVATO</td><td>3</td><td>3</td><td>6</td><td>9</td><td>12</td><td>15</td></tr>
<tr><td>ATTENZIONE</td><td>2</td><td>2</td><td>4</td><td>6</td><td>8</td><td>10</td></tr>
<tr><td>BASSO</td><td>1</td><td>1</td><td>2</td><td>3</td><td>4</td><td>5</td></tr>
</table>

Matrix of the RISK

Risk Assessment

Various definitions of risk types are also given, and we link them, for example, to the activity of skydiving, which is intrinsically a dangerous sport.

"Known" Risk

A real risk, quite well known and independent of the will of those who suffer it. A sports skydiver has a known risk.

"Unexpected" Risk

A risk that we do not expect (not foreseen), of which we have no experience, for which we are not culturally equipped. A parachute malfunction that has not been assessed is an unexpected risk.

"Accepted" Risk

A risk that is accepted to achieve a greater goal. For example, a "special forces" operator on a mission agrees with the risk and is aware of it but accepts it because he must achieve his objective at all costs.

"Sought" Risk

It is actively sought out for fun. For example, if the height is minimal, the parachutist does a base jump without a reserve parachute (which is not needed).

Therefore, the Italian "client" company has an obligation to guarantee the psycho-physical health of the worker on business 24 hours a day, even outside working hours.

The rules currently in force in Italy:

Legislative Decree 81/2008 (Consolidated law on health and safety at work)

Art.17 Obligations of the Employer that cannot be delegated.

The employer cannot delegate the following activities:

• Evaluation of all risks with the following elaboration of the document required by article 2823.

• The designation of the person responsible for the risk prevention and protection service.

• Art. 28 – Object of the Risk Assessment

"…..1. The assessment referred to in Article 17, paragraph 1, letter a), also in the choice of work equipment and the chemical substances or mixtures used, as well as in the arrangement of workplaces, must concern all risks to the safety and health of workers, including those concerning groups of exposed workers to particular risks, including those linked to work-related stress…

Legally speaking, we talk about "fault."

Legislative Decree 231/2001

Administrative responsibility of companies and bodies

Art. 4 c.1 – Crimes committed abroad

In the cases and under the conditions provided for by articles 7,8,9 and 10 of the penal code, entities having their main headquarters in the territory of the State are also liable in relation to crimes committed abroad, provided that the State of the place does not take action against them in which the crime was committed.

Article 25-septies.

Manslaughter and serious or very serious negligent injury committed in violation of the regulations on the protection of health and safety at work.

Legislative Decree 151/15

Working conditions of Italian workers to be employed or transferred abroad.

Article 16

"….The employment contract of Italian workers to be employed or transferred abroad provides insurance for each trip to the place of destination and return from the place itself, in cases of death or permanent disability; the type of logistical arrangement, appropriate safety measures…."

The word "SECURITY" is also used in other Latin-based languages, such as Spanish "Seguridad" or Portuguese "Segurança," which gives rise to a misinterpretation.

We must distinguish between "SAFETY" and "SECURITY".

Therefore, "SAFETY" concerns include fire prevention regulations, accident prevention, occupational doctors, personal protective equipment, etc.

Lack of SATETY causes » GUILT.

"SECURITY" refers to all exogenous risks, i.e., those risks that come from outside the work environment, such as criminal actions, kidnappings, terrorist attacks, and criminal acts. Therefore, situations external to the company.

These factors depend on the country, the time of year during which the trip occurs, the geopolitical conditions at that time, forecasts for the situation during the trip, and any local commemorations that might lead to unrest or riots. Choice of hotel or compound in the factory, choice of the route between factory and hotel and vice versa, etc…

Lack of SECURITY causes » FRAUD.

Furthermore, when a worker goes to another country, that country's "safety" regulations must be respected. Let me explain with an example: In Italy, safety shoes have a steel toe cap inside; in Brazil, for example, the toe cap is prohibited in production lines where there are electrical panels and must be replaced by one made of hard rubber to avoid any electric arcs at the feet.

There is a fundamental problem: How do we interpret the word security when a company sends one of its representatives abroad?

Here, we start talking about "SECURITY," which is much more complex than "SAFETY."

Choose how to organize the trip, airline, arrival and departure time, possible armed escort, what characteristics the escort must have, the location of the company where our employee will go to work, the hotel-factory route, a possible evacuation plan, etc. It can be deduced that the variables concerning security are much more complex than safety.

We give a classic definition of the concept of "COMPANY SECURITY" (External Security):

"Corporate SECURITY is the subject that studies develops, and implements strategies and operational plans to prevent or overcome events that can damage company resources over the course of an organization's life."

Therefore, this argument presupposes what is known in jurisprudence as "DOLO;" that is, it presumes that someone deliberately wants to cause damage." Hence, we deduce that what distinguishes "SAFETY" from "SECURITY" can be summarized with a third word, that is, "INTENTION" to cause harm on the part of someone, which is physical, image, psychological, etc.

How should a company organize itself to send a business traveler abroad?

First of all, you must contact a certified figure who is the SECURITY MANAGER ISO/UNI 10459 and/or SECURITY TRAVEL UNI/PDR 124/22 update. 12.09.2023

The functions of these professionals are the management of all the security processes of a company, which they tend to safeguard through the use of resources and tools of various kinds and, in the best conditions of cost, the company's assets against the losses that may affect it in carrying out its business." In the specific case that concerns a trip, essentially 6 things will have to be done:

1- DVR (risk validation document)

2- COUNTRY SHEET

3- INFORMATION

4- TRAINING

5- MONITORING

6- FINAL DEBRIEFING

1. DVR (Risk Assessment Document)

The DVR is the document that describes risks and prevention measures for health and safety in the workplace. DVR stands for Risk Assessment Document. This is a mandatory document (provided for by the Consolidated Law on safety at work) that identifies the risks present in a workplace and analyzes, evaluates, and tries to prevent dangerous situations for workers.

The Risk Assessment Document is mandatory for all businesses with at least one employee and for companies. The Consolidated Law on Health and Safety in the Workplace (Legislative Decree no. 81 of 2008) establishes that the DVR must be drawn up by the employer with the help of the Head of the Prevention and Protection Service (RSPP) and the doctor after consulting the Workers' Representative for Safety (RLS/RLST) where elected.

Legislative Decree. 81/08 – Consolidated law on health and safety at work requires the employer to train and inform its staff on all the possible risks they could face, including the so-called atypical exogenous risks, i.e., those types of risk that do not originate in the tasks performed.

2087, Civil Code – states that the entrepreneur must adopt the measures which, according to the particularity of the work, experience, and technique, are necessary to protect the workers' physical integrity and moral personality. It is about ensuring compliance with the set of provisions or measures necessary according to the work, experience, and technique to avoid or reduce professional risks in compliance with the health of the population and the integrity of the external environment.

Legislative Decree 8 June 2001, n. 231/01 states:

Article 4 – Crimes committed abroad, paragraph 1: "[...] bodies having their main headquarters in the territory of the State are also liable concerning crimes committed abroad [...]";

Article 25-septies: "Manslaughter or serious or very serious injuries committed in violation of the regulations on the protection of health and safety at work."

Legislative Decree 15 September 2015, n. 151 Article 18 – Working conditions of Italian workers to be employed or transferred abroad states:

The employment contract of Italian workers to be employed or transferred abroad provides insurance for each trip to the place of destination and return from the place itself in cases of death or permanent disability.

The type of logistical arrangement » suitable safety measures.»

2. THE COUNTRY SHEET

The evaluation of the country sheet must first be done by obtaining information from the Ministry of Foreign Affairs and Economic Development's website. It is also a good idea to check the website of the Swiss Federal Department of Foreign Affairs

(DFA). It would be advisable for the company to sign an annual contract with an international provider (generally English, American, or French companies), which provides the geopolitical situation of any country in real time. It is good practice to create a series of contacts over time with security managers who work locally in various countries to obtain updated, firsthand information. Generally, the study of the country card is carried out 1 month before the traveler's departure and updated a couple of days before.

3. INFORMATION

Travel risks have various facets, from missing a flight with consequent change in arrival time and date (it is necessary to notify the hotel, escort, and the person waiting at the airport (also called "fixer"). A good rule is always (apart from booking the hotel) to have information on the availability of a "reserve" hotel, as the booked hotel might be unavailable due to any weather or other event.

Regarding the person waiting at the airport in the arrivals area with the classic sign where the traveler's name is written, you have to (and I say this from experience) be a little careful. First of all, it may happen that during baggage sorting at the arrival airport, an attacker communicates your name via mobile phone to a colleague in the arrivals hall. The latter identifies the person holding the sign with the traveler's name and makes him leave the room with an excuse. At this point, he puts himself in a position not to cause harm and replaces himself with the sign waiting for the unsuspecting traveler, who is tired from the several hours of travel and can't wait to go to the hotel. Therefore, he does not check on the true identity of the person. The company that sends the worker abroad must previously send a copy of the documents of the person who will receive the traveler at the airport. The latter must check them carefully (which is apparently trivial, but if you are in Africa, where a slightly blurry photo of a black person can easily be confused with another person, or in China, where they all have almond-shaped eyes, this can cause problems. It should also be noted that generally, if you arrive from a flight lasting several hours without having slept, your mind is unclear, and you will be so tired that you can't wait to go to the hotel. First of all, the traveler must always ask the name of the hotel where he is going to stay and must wait for a correct answer, and not say it himself! The safest thing is to have it sent away before the trip. E-mail a "password" that those who are waiting must know based on a specific question!

If there is something that does not match, the traveler absolutely must not leave the airport and call the Italian company, which will activate the local customer. It goes without saying that having a mobile phone working while roaming and/or using a satellite phone is essential.

Classic sign at the airport reception...but will they be the real ones?

4. TRAINING

"Elicitation" should also be included in the training; it involves collecting information from personal and professional contact that is characterized by developing a human relationship that supports the use of discreet conversational manipulation. It is a complex of activities that involve:

–   Basic understanding of human nature

–   Knowledge of techniques that make contacts likely to make information

–   Practical experience in interpersonal communication

–   When you are the target of a hostile elicitor, what you DON'T say is just as important as what you say.

The first step you need to understand is why you are a target.

– Consider the following questions:

– What critical information do you need to protect?

– Why do you need to protect them?

– Who do you want to protect them from?

– If you are asked for specific information, how do you respond?

The training of a travel worker is fundamental and concerns many aspects. Knowing local customs can avoid embarrassing situations and loss of credibility; for example, extending your hand to greet a woman in an Islamic country is inappropriate.

During Ramadan, when those who respect it locally do not drink, smoke, or eat from sunrise to sunset, it is customary not to do so for the traveler in the presence of local staff. A minimum of confidentiality is essential to prevent misunderstandings that could damage working relationships and not affect what the English call "business continuity."

It also depends on the country and, specifically, which city you are in; if you are in Istanbul, Turkey, it is not the same as being in Sarliufa on the border with Syria, where the local population is much more intransigent. For example, despite the 50° centigrade in Saudi Arabia, you cannot enter a shopping center in shorts or even get on a plane like that. Or mistakenly queuing at a McDonald's in the lane reserved for women and families. While the consumption of alcohol is strictly prohibited in Saudi Arabia, in Dubai, you can drink, purchase, and transport alcohol; theoretically, it is necessary to have an "alcohol license."

"Locals" are absolutely prohibited from consuming. Expats and tourists, on the other hand, have different solutions designed especially for the millions of tourists who arrive in the city every year. In fact, it is possible to drink alcohol, even without a license, inside structures such as hotels and restaurants (which have the relevant permit).

In Dubai, there is "Sharia Law" that mandates it is not possible to consume alcohol on the street or in public places. Naturally, you need to look at this law with a keen eye to understand it fully. What is forbidden for expats and tourists (rightly so) is abuse. If, in our country, those who exaggerate too much get away with having a bouncer accompany them to the door, the consequences can be severe in Dubai: they risk arrest and very high fines.

So let's say that there are two fundamental rules to remember to avoid having problems:

- Respect

- Common sense

Respect is crucial; as the proverb goes, "When in Rome, do as the Romans do," which means adapting to the customs of the place you're in. Remember, you're in someone else's house, and it's important to honor their traditions and culture. As another saying puts it, "When you're in someone else's house, you must do as they do." Yes, "indulgence" would be a more precise term if you're specifically referring to the overuse or excessive enjoyment of things like alcohol, food, or other behaviors. "Indulgence" conveys the idea of giving in to excess or luxury, which fits well with the context of respecting local customs and avoiding problematic behaviors.

Common sense is crucial because excessive indulgence can lead to dangerous situations for oneself and others, regardless of where you are. This principle applies universally. For instance, Dubai is known for its tolerance, but visitors should not take this leniency for granted.

A few years ago, while traveling to Riyadh, Saudi Arabia, I took a flight to visit a client in Dammam on the Persian Gulf. As soon as I settled into my seat, a hostess politely asked me to stand up, collect my hand luggage, and proceed to the finger— a device connecting the plane to the terminal—where I was met by the Islamic religious police, known as the "Mutaww'a."

A person dressed in classic dress was waiting for me in a black "kaftan" and told me that according to Islamic religious law, I could not travel by plane in shorts (I had shorts that reached my knees! But, there was no point in arguing since it was customary that way there). I told him it would have been no problem if they had brought me the suitcase that had been loaded onto the plane earlier, as I could have changed into a more appropriate dress. The "Mutaww'a" didn't consider where and how I would change. To do so, I would have had to go to the toilet outside the finger, which could have made me miss the flight. It came to me at the right time, and then the classic Italian imagination came into play…

A few days ago, at the hotel, I met a local gentleman who came to the hotel every weekend with his family; one day, he gave me a white kaftan (classic Arab dress), complete with kufiyya (veil), as a warm gesture.

In order for me to change, the flight had to wait 30 minutes for my suitcase to be brought to me. I opened the suitcase and put on the kaftan and kufiyya over the t-shirt and shorts to the amazement of the hostesses, passengers, and Mutawwa'a himself, who also complimented me, but on the inside, I clearly told him to go to hell.

A classic application of "Awareness," i.e., the understanding and knowledge of local habits and customs that must be taught during the training course of a travel worker.

Arabic style arriving at Damman airport (Saudi Arabia)

Damman, located in the Persian Gulf, is also in Saudi territory and is connected by a bridge called "King Fahd," it is 25 km long in Bahrain. In the Middle of this bridge is the Saudi Arabia-Barhain border. In the same hotel, a group of German technicians who, one Friday evening, were eager to drink a few mugs of beer since Bahrain is "alcohol-free" crossed the bridge entering Bahrain territory.

They were supposed to return the next day, but I didn't see them for a week! So what had happened?

The German company that employed them clearly provided them with a single-entry visa for Saudi Arabia, not a multiple-entry visa. As a result, once they crossed the border into Bahrain, they were unable to return to Saudi Arabia.

They had to wait a few days to make an appointment at the Saudi embassy in Bahrain to get another visa to return to Damman. As a result, on top of additional costs of food and accommodation in Bahrain, they created a loss of reputation for their company towards the customer and also a loss of "business continuity."

Furthermore, keep in mind that when dealing with bank transactions with or within Islamic countries, the public holiday is Friday, and the pre-holiday is Thursday, which would correspond to our Sunday and Saturday, respectively. Banks in the West work on Monday, Tuesday, Wednesday, Thursday, and Friday, while in the Islamic countries, they work on Saturday, Sunday, Monday, Tuesday, and Wednesday.

Result: the working days in which European banks will be able to exchange bank transfers with one from Saudi Arabia or other Islamic countries will be only 3, i.e., Monday, Tuesday, and Wednesday (and not 5 as we do in Europe or the USA), this leads to delays in bank transactions even with a "wire transfer" (immediate bank transfer).

5. MONITORING

Depending on the risk assessment outlined in the DVR (Document of Risk Assessment) for a given country, if it's deemed that the traveler can only leave the hotel to go to work or if a specific hotel-to-work route has been established for the trip, the traveler must be monitored 24/7. The traveler will have signed a document during the training course acknowledging this requirement and must be aware of the conditions. This presupposes that in Italy, 2 or 3 people in shifts continuously check the traveler's movements.

Here, we enter into a "privacy" topic that the employee could contest against the employer, but I think that at a certain point, the location of the employee is more important for his safety than his "privacy," but this is an entirely subjective opinion.

The employee could install a "spoofing" program on his mobile phone, which forces the position transmitted by WhatsApp wherever he wants, but it only works if the "current" position is transmitted, not the "real-time" one.

GPS "spoofing," in other words, forces the phone to transmit a false position with respect to where it is located.

- The first solution is to provide the traveler with a company telephone where no further programs can be installed.

- The second solution is inherent in these "spoofing" programs; once activated, the "real-time position" is deactivated, and only the "current" position is transmitted; a typical program could be "iAnyGo."

There is a very simple method to understand if a "spoofing" program has been activated on the phone: to have the person move even just 100 meters; if the phone transmits the movement, everything is ok; otherwise, "spoofing" has been activated.

6. FINAL DEBRIEFING

The term "Debriefing" refers to the reverse analysis process that is carried out at the end of the trip and allows us to verify the actual achievement of the objectives and evaluate the critical issues that arose during the trip. In light of the new experience, the "Travel Security Manager" will have to update the country card, keeping in mind that the situation may be completely different with each new trip.

ISO 31030:2021

ISO 31030 is a high-level standard for companies aiming to anticipate and evaluate the possible risks of travel; the ISO fills the regulatory gap left in jobs carried out abroad by assisting the employer in making informed decisions based on risk assessments and solid methodologies along with updated and exhaustive information.

The ISO standard is mainly made up of four points:

1. Scope, context, and risk criteria. Define and integrate the scope and objectives of the risk management program, ensuring your workforce can travel and work in a safe and secure environment and have systems in place to help deal with emergencies.

2. Travel risk assessment and management process - Travel Risk Assessment. Identify, analyze, mitigate, and manage all risks likely to impact, directly or indirectly, a business trip's smooth and peaceful conduct. In this regard, it is essential to clearly establish roles and responsibilities and outline a clear and well-defined process based on a careful evaluation of the principal risk factors and correct and effective identification and implementation of the relevant countermeasures.

3. Travel and operational management. Effectively implement appropriate risk management processes and measures. The Travel Risk Policy, integrated according to the indications of the

4. https://www.ambimed-group.com/it/iso-31030-dal-travel-risk-management-alla-valuazione-dei-rischi
standard, must be effectively communicated within the company in order to increase the awareness of the traveling workforce, also by resorting to an efficient, clear, and immediate training strategy;

5. Recording and reporting. Activate a system that allows you to review the effectiveness of your travel management

program on a regular basis. The monitoring and collection of information and the use of technology must allow for a continuous review of the process to evaluate its effectiveness and compliance with any changing needs.

The Travel Risk Assessment

The process to guarantee the safety of travelers is diversified, and a fundamental stage is the Travel Risk Assessment, that is, the evaluation of travel risks. It consists of a detailed analysis of the potential risks and threats that travelers may encounter during their travels, both nationally and internationally. The main objective of the Travel Risk Assessment is to identify and evaluate factors that may put the safety, health, and well-being of travelers at risk in order to take the necessary measures to mitigate these risks.

The travel risk assessment can include several components, including:

1. Travel destination: the analysis of the political situation, security conditions, health risks, weather conditions, and other local factors that could influence the safety of travelers is essential;

2. Analysis of critical issues: an analysis is carried out of potential critical issues that may arise during the trip, such as terrorism, crime, road accidents, natural disasters, or health emergencies;

3. Profile of travelers: it is vital to take into consideration the profile of travelers, such as age, gender, travel experience, special needs, and past medical history;

4. Means of transport: safety statistics, the reliability of transport service providers, and the potential risks associated with each means are taken into consideration;

5. Medical and health services: the quantity and quality of local health facilities, emergency services, recommended vaccinations, and preventive measures for travelers' health are evaluated.

Il Travel Risk Manager UNI/PDR 124/22 agg. 12.09.2023

The travel risk manager is a professional dedicated to the safety and well-being of corporate travelers. This figure is crucial in ensuring that appropriate measures are taken to protect workers during their travels and effectively manage emergency situations that may arise.

The responsibilities of a travel risk manager may include:

• Risk assessment: it is responsible for conducting in-depth assessments of potential travel risks, including with the help of external partners.

• Policy and Procedure Development: Develops and implements policies, procedures, and guidelines to ensure traveler safety.

• Monitoring and alerting: maintains constant monitoring of local conditions and emerging threats.

- Training and awareness: provides training and orientation to travelers on the importance of travel safety and the preventive measures to be taken.

- Emergency management: in the event of crisis situations or emergencies during travel, the travel risk manager coordinates the activation of emergency plans, the organization of the evacuation of travelers, and communication with the competent authorities.

In an increasingly globalized and complex world, addressing travel-related risks requires careful planning, assessing potential dangers, and managing unexpected situations. Integrating travel risk management into company policies helps preserve the company's reputation and reduce the potential financial impact of emergencies.

However, it is necessary to remember that traveler safety is a shared responsibility between individuals, organizations, and competent authorities. We can only create a safer travel environment and protect the lives and well-being of workers venturing into foreign lands by collaborating and working together.

The Stakeholders involved during commissioning abroad

The Internal Team

People and departments involved in organizing a trip

- TOP Management;

- Branch Managers;

• HR (Human Resources)

• Business Units;

• QHSE (Quality, Health, Safety, and Environment Manager)

• Procurement;

• Security;

• Risk Management;

• Travel Management;

• Logistics

• Finance

• Commercial and Marketing

• Training department;

The External Team

People and external service providers are involved in the organization of a voyage.

• Insurance;

• Embassies and consulates;

• Crisis unit;

• Travel agencies;

• Private Security Companies;

Risk Management Process

(Risk Assessment)

Systematic and overall process of evaluating the effects of uncertainty for achieving an objective.

• RISK IDENTIFICATION: the process of determining what risks are expected, their characteristics, time dependencies, frequencies, duration period, and possible outcomes.

• RISK ANALYSIS: process to characterize, understand, and define the level of risk.

• RISK ASSESSMENT: Process of equating risk analysis results with risk criteria to determine whether a particular level of risk is within an acceptable tolerance and the organization is capable of managing it.

I bring these 3 concepts back to my trip to Baghdad as an example I spoke about in Chapter 2.

The "Risk Identification" had to be done clearly before my departure by a travel risk company, which should have analyzed the situation in Baghdad a few weeks before and subsequently even a few days before.

To get first-hand news, you can turn to reliable local contacts or "international providers," to which you have to subscribe at a very variable cost depending on the number of countries and the level of information you want. They can provide an analysis of the most reliable airlines, safe hotels, optimal hotel-factory routes, lists of PSCs (Private Security Companies) with verified licenses, characteristics of their operators, daily costs, evacuation plans from the factory, hotels, etc.

In my case, only a 2-hour course was held, and a remote consultancy company did a very general "induction," which was useless in practice.

The "Risk Analysis," i.e., determining the risk "R" through the risk matrix (see page 123), was not even taken into consideration; therefore, neither the probability nor the impact was assessed, and consequently, neither the risk (R=P*I).

The "Risk Assessment" was non-existent because if there were no risk analysis, there would not be a risk assessment.

The threat: an unexpected event that can represent a danger to the asset (person, property, system, environment, community).

We can divide the various types of threats into:

CRIME

• ORGANIZED OR COMMON

• PIRACY

• SMUGGLING

• PREDATORY CRIMES OF A SEXUAL NATURE

WAR/TERRORISTIC

• ETHNIC-RELIGIOUS

• ENDOGENOUS, EXOGENOUS

• REGIONAL

- ANTI-Western

- CONFLICTS

POLITICAL/SOCIAL

- CORRUPTION

- EXPLOITATION

- VIOLENCE IN THE WORKPLACE

- ALCOHOL OR DRUG ABUSE

ANTHROPIC/ENVIRONMENTAL

- INDUSTRIAL AREAS

- POLLUTION

- NATURAL EVENTS

- CLIMATIC CONDITIONS

- SANITARY AND HYGIENIC CONDITIONS

- ILLNESSES

In my opinion, an interesting concept is "ACCEPTABLE RISK"; it happens when probability and impact vary, and the risk remains "constant" and lower than a predetermined value.

The function P x I = Constant is represented by the hyperbolic curve in the figure:

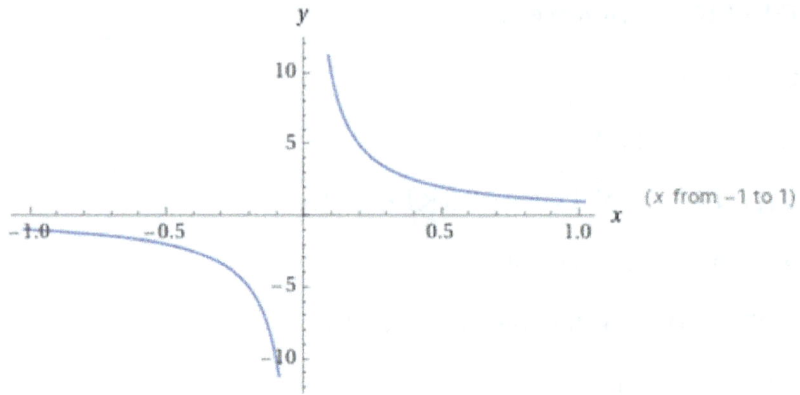

We consider the curve only for x>0 where x=Probability and y=Impact.

Any point belonging to the curve has the product (i.e., the risk R) of its coordinates constant.

In the case of the figure, the risk R=P*I=1

In this other case, R=P*I=10; therefore, the acceptance of the risk is greater than that of the previous one!

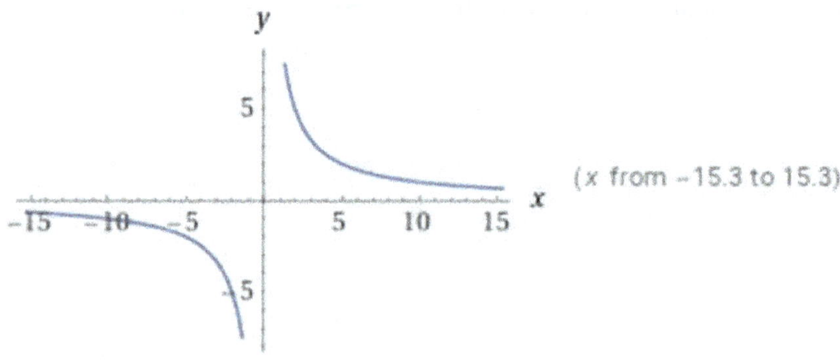

CHAPTER 7: CURRENT SITUATION

Everything I described in the previous chapter (Chapter 6) is thoroughly researched and then written, but it must be applied by companies who must also make their employees aware. It will remain a pure and beautiful academic theory if this doesn't happen!

When I talk about these topics with an entrepreneur who has business travelers abroad, 90% of them give me 2 answers, and 10% fall on the other side:

1. It hasn't happened to me that one of my employees was harmed, kidnapped, injured, or worse, by an exogenous event, i.e., external to the company or internationally. In other words, they play on probability, the law of large numbers.

2. We, as a company, are insured!

To the first answer, I respond like this: But if it happens to you and the company has not taken precautions, there will be pain and penalties from an administrative and criminal point of view.

To the second I answer: insurance companies know the laws very well, and before paying, they will check whether you have complied with Legislative Decree 81/2008 and Legislative Decree 231/2008. If you haven't done so, they will never pay.

In reality, Legislative Decree 81/2008 was created to enact workplace safety, above all, to drastically reduce the approximately 1200 deaths at work that we also had in 2023 due to endogenous causes, certainly not due to terrorist attacks and/or kidnappings of business travelers. The latter, even if to an extremely lesser extent, a few units annually, receive much more media attention than the 1200 workplace deaths a year also because, when they do happen, they often involve high-profile responses such as interventions from the Farnesina crisis unit, our external services (AISE), perhaps a Government Falcon jet that goes to bring the kidnapped person back to his homeland.

I remember that in seventh grade (it was still called that), the history teacher asked the following question:

What did the ancient Romans introduce as new compared to other peoples?

These were the most disparate answers:

The roads, the bridges, the organization of the army, etc.

The answer I gave was: *"THE WRITTEN LAWS";* in fact, no people at that time had written laws.

Now, we Italians, heirs of this Roman empire, which was the first to make written laws, have no system for checking and balancing written laws, but in the case of the topic I am dealing with, the vast majority of entrepreneurs, especially SMEs (small medium enterprises) who send employees travel abroad even though they know that they must comply with Legislative Decree 81/2008 and Legislative Decree 231/2001, they do not do so for the simple reason that there are no controls.

Out of curiosity, I called SPISAL (Workplace Hygiene Protection Service) on the phone in Rome and asked to speak to a manager. I asked him why, despite numerous safety inspections, I see many checks on your part but absolutely nothing regarding security. The response was that SPISAL officials are not trained to check DVRs, country cards, training, and information, i.e., everything related to security. Maybe I had talked to the wrong person!

These are just some cases of Italians kidnapped abroad in recent years:

Alessandro Sandrini

In May 2016, Alessandro Sandrini, who had been kidnapped by a criminal gang on the border between Syria and Turkey, was released. At the time of his release, Sandrini was one of eight Italian citizens whose traces had been lost in recent years and who were still missing, probably kidnapped by criminal or jihadist groups. Since then, there has been no release, either through operations by the security forces or after ransom payment. Today, there are seven Italians kidnapped abroad and still kidnapped: a tourist, an aid worker, three traders, and two priests. There is no certain news about them, although the Foreign Ministry continues to work to obtain their release.

Paolo Dall'Oglio

The priest Paolo Dall'Oglio was kidnapped in Raqqa, Syria, on 29 July 2013, perhaps by some ISIS militiamen. Before the kidnapping, Dall'Oglio, 64 years old, had lived in Syria for almost thirty years and was known for having re-founded the Syriac Catholic monastic community of Mar Musa, north of Damascus: he had been expelled from the country in 2011 on the orders of Bashar al Assad's regime, which had targeted him for meeting opposition activists, but he returned in 2013. In recent years, several sources have claimed that Dall'Oglio was killed, but the news has never been confirmed: in February, the Times wrote that he was still alive.

Silvia Romano

Silvia Romano, a 23-year-old volunteer of Milanese origins, was kidnapped on 19 November 2018 in the village of Chakama in southern Kenya, where she was on behalf of an Italian non-profit organization. A group of common criminals carried out the kidnapping. It is suspected that Romano was sold to another gang of robbers in December. Silvia was freed on Saturday, 9 May, in an area not far from Mogadishu, with an operation by the Aise, the Italian external intelligence services, conducted in collaboration with the Turkish and Somali ones. In the aftermath of the kidnapping, the local police had hypothesized that the kidnapping was the work of common criminals for the purpose of extortion but had not excluded the possibility that the volunteer could be taken across the border to Somalia to be handed over to the Al-Arab rebels. Shabaab, who controls parts of Somali territory. Last November, following the arrest of three of those responsible for the kidnapping, confirmation came that the girl had been transferred to a Somali jihadist group. From that moment on, nothing more had been heard of Silvia Romano. Today, some aspects of the circumstances of his release raise questions about the changed geopolitical and strategic balances in the Horn of Africa.

Luca Tacchetto

Luca Tacchetto, a 30-year-old architect originally from Vigonza, in the province of Padua, was kidnapped in Burkina Faso last December 2018 together with Canadian Edith Blais. The two had left Europe by car and were headed to Togo to collaborate as volunteers in the construction of a village. They disappeared on December 15th, after Tacchetto and Blais had spent the evening with Robert Guilloteau, a French friend of theirs. Last April, a Burkina Faso minister told Rai News 24 that Tacchetto and Pier Luigi Maccalli, another kidnapped Italian, were alive but no longer in the country. The Human Rights Watch organization claimed that Tacchetto and Blais were taken to Mali. Released in March 2020.

Pier Luigi Maccalli

Pier Luigi Maccalli, originally from Madignano (province of Cremona), was kidnapped in Niger on the night between 17 and 18 September 2018, when he was a missionary of the Society of African Missions. The kidnapping took place in Bomoanga, on the border between Niger and Burkina Faso: according to reconstructions in recent months, Maccalli was first robbed, then put in a car by his kidnappers and taken to Burkina Faso. It is unknown where he is now. According to the Burkina Faso minister who spoke to Rainews last April, he would have been brought back to Niger, but there is no confirmation. He was released in October 2020.

Raffaele Russo, Antonio Russo and Vincenzo Cimmino

Raffaele Russo, his son Antonio, and his nephew Vincenzo Cimmino have been missing in Mexico since January 31, 2018. The three Italians, originally from Naples, were street vendors and disappeared in Tecalitlán, a city of 16 thousand inhabitants about 600 kilometers west of Mexico City. There is still no news of the three today. Four policemen were indicted for their kidnapping, including a woman, who confessed to Mexican magistrates that they had sold the hostages to a criminal gang from Tecalitlán.

BONATTI S.P.A. CASE

The Bonatti case concerns the kidnapping of four company technicians during an overland transfer in Libya to reach their workplace. During the journey, they are kidnapped, and during the firefight that takes place at the time of the liberation attempt, two of them are killed. The Italian embassy had advised against the transfer by land, suggesting, precisely because of the terrorist risk, travel by sea from the island of Djerba in Tunisia. However, for company reasons, it was decided to ignore the suggestion. The criminal action of the Rome Public Prosecutor's Office was inspired by this affair, resulting in the sentence of the GUP of

Rome in January 2016. The Roman Judicial Authority at the same time orders - with this sentence - the sentence of 1 year and 10 months to the president of the Bonatti, Paolo Ghirelli, and two members of the Board of Directors of the same, Dino Martinazzoli and Paolo Cardano (who have chosen to be judged with abbreviated proceedings) for negligent cooperation in the intentional crime, as well as, with the same provision, condemns the Bonatti company to a fine of €150,000 pursuant to art. 25-septies of Legislative Decree 231/2001 on the administrative liability of entities, also providing compensation to the families of the victims of €150,000; furthermore, it commits the third member of the Bonatti Board, Giovanni Di Vincenzo, to trial for the same crime and accepts the request for a plea bargain of 1 year and 10 months of Bonatti's manager in Libya, Dennis Morson. From a legislative point of view, the "Bonatti sentence" introduced the concept of "culpable cooperation in an intentional crime" into jurisprudence.

From a political point of view, the Legislative Decree should be amended. 81/2008 in order to make it clear in detail what the company's legal manager must do and which staff he must contact to do this.

Currently, companies are required by law to have an RSPP internally or externally, depending on the number of employees. However, the current law does not oblige them to have an ISO/UNI 10459 certified "security manager" and a UNI/"Travel Risk

Manager." PDR 124/22 updated. 12.09.2023 nor to follow the ISO/UNI 31030 regulatory letter.

The Friuli Venezia Giulia region has finally officially recognized the figure of the security manager in some sectors. Article 52 of the regional law of 3 March 2023 of the Friuli Venezia Giulia region refers to the "Regional Security Manager for regional critical infrastructures," compliant with the UNI 10459 standard, duly certified. I would say, "ONE SMALL STEP FORWARD!"

CHAPTER 8

An example of an "Awareness Form" that the traveler must sign.

SECURITY AWARENESS FORM

The undersigned ……………., employee of the company or consultant ………………., declares that on date …………… carried out the Security Awareness Induction for the trip to XXXX for the customer XXXXX and to have received the following documents simultaneously to the following e-mail address XXXXXXXXXX Travel Risk Guide and Health Risk Guide, and that you have participated in the course on safety and security aspects of travel, including local customs, entry requirements, and related security risks specifically to the destination of your trip. The undersigned recognizes the importance of adhering to all guidelines and security protocols provided by the Travel Security Team to ensure their safety and undertakes to follow these recommendations both on the production site during working hours and externally over time free.

The undersigned undertakes to avoid any dangerous behavior or activity that could endanger his well-being, compromise his personal safety, or damage the "business continuity" of the company.

You must contact the Travel Security Team for any request for clarification on the trip at the following e-mail address: XXXXXXXXX or at the following numbers:

XXXXXX, XXXXXX, XXXXX

Date and signature:

NB: this document is sent and signed via e-mail to the following address: XXXXXXXXX

AN EXAMPLE OF TRAVEL GUIDE "TURKEY"

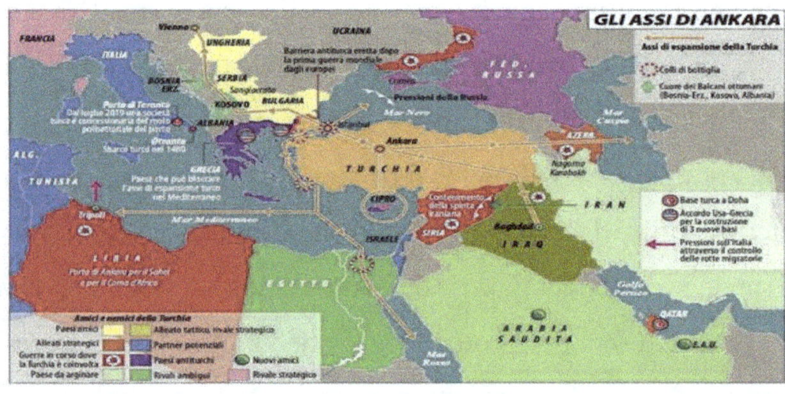

County: **Turkey**

Last update: 25/04/2024

(two days before departure)

1 Introduction

2 In short

3 Terrorism

4 Crime

5 Politics and Society

6 Ethics

7 Transport

7.1 Air Transport

7.2 Road Routes

8 Safety precautions

9 Cultural Indications

10 Business information

Turkish Lira Currency (TRY) 1 EUR = 33.2647 TRY 1 USD = 30.8759 TRY

Documents Passport validity: 6 months

Visa: For information, visit the Turkish Ministry of Foreign Affairs website or contact the consular authorities.

Various Official language(s): Turkish. Other languages: English (a little), German

Currency: Turkish Lira, TRY (1 EUR = 33.2647 TRY;

1 USD = 30.8759 TRY)

Other currencies: Euro (EUR), US Dollar (USD)

Time Zone(s): UTC +3 Daylight Saving Time: Not adopted.

Capital: Ankara

Religion: Muslims 99.8% (a clear majority of Sunnis), other confessions 0.2%

Government: Presidential Republic

President: Recep Tayyip Erdogan

Emergency numbers: The following emergency numbers are active in the country: 112, ambulance; 110, firefighters; 155/154, police. Airports New Airport

Istanbul International, Istanbul (IST); Sabiha Gokcen

International Airport, Istanbul - Asian side (SAW); Esenboğa, Ankara (ESB); Adnan Menderes, Izmir (ADB); Adana/Sakirpasa, Adana (ADA); Antalya (AYT); Dalaman (DLM). Ports Istanbul Mersin, Izmir, Eregli, Samsun. Ankara Railways, Haydarpaşa Terminal (Istanbul, European Side), Sirkeci Terminal (Istanbul, European Side), Bostanci (Istanbul, Asian Side), Izmir, Izmit, Kars, Mersin.

Embassy Italian Embassy in ANKARA Ataturk Bulvari n. 118 06680 Kavaklidere Ankara, Türkiye Tel.: +90 312

4574200; Fax: +90 312 4574280; Sales Office Tel. +90 312 4574275; Sales Office Fax +90 312 4574282.

E-mail: umba.ankara@esteri.itassociazione. ankara@esteri.it website: https://ambankara.esteri.it/imba_ankara/it/ Consular Chancellery c/o

Embassy in Ankara E-mail Consular Chancellery: consolare.ambankara@esteri.it

Fax Consular Registry +90 312 4574281

On public holidays and in the evenings of weekdays, in cases of actual emergency, the following numbers are active:

For the Ankara and Cappadocia area:

+90 532 374 8177 -

For the Istanbul area and the Black Sea coast:

+90 555 458 5844 -

For the Izmir area, the Mediterranean coast, and the south-east of Turkey: +90 532 6773273 On-call mobile, only in emergency cases, active 24 hours a day on closing days +90 5340743363

Consulate General of Italy in Istanbul Tom Tom Kaptan Sokak, 5 - 34433 Beyoglu, Istanbul Tel: 0090 212 2431024/5, 2525437, 2513294 Fax: 0090 212 2525879 Consulate General availability in Istanbul: 0090-555-4585844 Homepage: https://consistanbul.esteri.it/consolato_ istanbul/it/ E-mail:

consolatogenerale.istanbul@esteri.it Consulate of Italy in Izmir Cumhuriyet Meydani, 12 35210 Izmir Tel +90 232 4636676 / 96 Fax +90 232 4212512 Contact cell of the Italian Consulate in Izmir: 0090- 532-6773273

e-mail: consolato.izmir@esteri.itconsolato.izmir@ Esteri.it website: https://consizmir.esteri.it/consolato_izmir/it

1. PREMISE

This document provides useful information to understand and mitigate the security risks present in the country. Implementing all the recommended measures must not exempt one from adopting behavior that always complies with the standard rules of diligence, prudence, and expertise. The document does not contain administrative or health advice and must be considered valid until new events change the security framework and the country's risk level. From the point of view of analysis and methodological approach, this document does not represent a risk assessment of the country. This guide, as required by internal provisions, is aimed at employees and/or consultants who go on business trips and has been prepared in compliance with current legislation and with particular reference to Legislative Decree 81/2008.

2. IN BRIEF

Turkey presents an extremely heterogeneous security picture. In particular, they represent areas at high risk for terrorism: the localities located less than 10 km from the border with Syria and the south-eastern provinces (in particular those of Sirnak, Diyarbakir, Kilis, Hatay, and Hakkari) and that of Tunceli. The numerous military operations launched by the Turkish government in northern Syria and Iraqi Kurdistan have also had repercussions on the security situation in the Turkish areas close to the border. In this regard, we note an increase in PKK actions in the areas bordering Syria, Iraq, and Iran. Again, with reference to terrorism, there is a deep-rooted presence in the territory of cells and networks attributable to the Islamic State (IS), especially in the areas adjacent to the Syrian border, as well as in the major cities of the country. Crime remains at low levels: the greatest risk for foreign staff is represented by petty crime, widespread in large cities, where pickpocketing and scams are relatively frequent. Protest demonstrations against the government and against US and Israeli embassies or consulates are possible, sometimes likely to degenerate into disorder and violence.

Further protest hotspots could be universities and universities in major urban centers, especially in Istanbul and Ankara. Due to the ongoing political tensions between opposition and government parties, there is a real risk of asymmetric actions perpetrated against buildings, individuals, and representatives of the country's main political parties. Turkey is exposed to a high seismic risk in the northeast and along the Tigris and Euphrates rivers. There are currently residual problems in numerous south-eastern areas of the country (provinces of Kahramanmaras, Adana, Adiyaman, Osmaniye, Hatay, Kilis, Malatya, Sanliurfa, Diyarbakir, and Gaziantep), hit in February 2023 by two violent earthquakes of magnitude 7.8 and 7.7. Follow the safety instructions in this document scrupulously and carefully.

3. TERRORISM

The terrorist phenomenon in Türkiye mainly has a dual matrix: Jihadist and Kurdish. As regards the jihadist terrorist threat, the presence of cells linked both to IS and other Salafist terrorist organizations remains firmly rooted in the territory. However, the threat has appeared to decrease compared to the two-year period 2015-2017. According to available information, the Turkish authorities 5 Travel Guide are monitoring more than 18,000 alleged individuals with links to IS. Furthermore, according to official sources, there are approximately 1,500 fighters of Turkish nationality who have gone to Syria and Iraq to fight in the ranks of IS and other jihadist groups. The persistence of the threat - even in the current context of strong instability in the entire Middle Eastern region connected to the conflict in the Gaza Strip - seemed confirmed by the recent attack against a Catholic Church in Istanbul (28 January 2024, 1 victim, claimed by IS). Finally, it should be noted that al-Qaeda factions in Syria could strike the country in response to the Turkish commitment in the Syrian scenario. However, currently, the main threat comes from the

Kurdish front. Within national borders, the groups TAK - Kurdistan Freedom Hawks - and PKK - Kurdistan Workers' Party - generally carry out attacks against the police and the army, trying to attack mainly barracks and checkpoints. Despite this, the possibility of indirect involvement of civilians during the carrying out of these attacks remains high. These formations are active mainly in southern Turkey (in the provinces of Hakkari, Sirnak, Diyarbakir, and Tunceli, and, to a lesser extent, Siirt, Mardin, Batman, and Agri). They can also carry out high-profile actions in cities such as Ankara and Istanbul. These formations usually use explosive devices (IED) and, in certain circumstances, may also resort to the use of suicidal actions, including by means of car bombs (SVBIED). It should also be noted that the PKK is reportedly increasing the scale of attacks perpetrated through the use of armed drones (UAVs). Attacks of the same type are possible near the main airport infrastructures, including civilian ones, in the south-east of the country, especially near the borders with Syria, Iraq, and Iran.

Furthermore, it is highlighted how the interests of the country, both abroad and on the national territory, can be the object of offensive actions perpetrated by groups gravitating in the anarchist area, both national (DHKP-C) and international (FAI-FRI), mainly in retaliation for Turkish intervention in Syrian Kurdistan. These actions are usually perpetrated against targets attributable to the defense and military technology sectors through the use of incendiary devices, especially at night. However, higher profile actions, such as the armed attack that occurred on February 6, 2024, at the Caglayan Court in Istanbul, are also possible. The attackers (based on what was ascertained by the Turkish authorities belonging to the DHKP-C) were neutralized by the security forces; the action caused 1 death and 6 injuries. On several occasions, Israeli authorities have signaled the risk of attacks against Israeli individuals and interests in Turkey, calling on citizens to leave the country (as occurred, for example, in October 2023).

4. CRIME

The worsening of socio-economic conditions recorded in recent years has led to an increase in the crime rate in Ankara, Istanbul, and Izmir compared to the other main urban centers of the country. However, criminal phenomena remain at lower overall levels than those recorded in Western cities of similar size. Violent crime is quite rare, and the main risks for business travelers arise from theft, snatching, and pickpocketing, which are more frequent in particularly crowded areas and tourist attraction areas such as Taksim Square, Sultanahmet, and near the Grand Bazaar and the Spice Bazaar (all in Istanbul). Criminals often use diversions (such as arguments, fights, and fights) to distract the intended victim. Thefts in apartments and hotels are constantly increasing (in particular, in those that use magnetic cards to access rooms). Although infrequent, car thefts have been reported in Istanbul and other areas of the country. Particular attention must be paid when operating ATMs, especially at night. Over the years, the number of sexual harassment and violence has increased significantly; this trend does not only indicate an aggravation of the phenomenon but also a greater willingness of victims to come forward. Sexual crimes, including rape, have been recorded, including against minors, especially at night in coastal tourist areas. The Turkish National Police has good levels of professionalism and adequate capabilities in combating crime. Kidnappings by Kurdish groups are quite frequent in the south-eastern area of the country but generally target soldiers or local personalities.

There is a current risk, throughout the national territory, of kidnappings of foreign personnel by IS and PKK militants looking for money to finance their actions. The threat of abduction is particularly high in the border areas with Syria. Kidnappings of foreign citizens are occasionally recorded, mostly by criminal groups and for the purpose of extortion, even in major urban centers (some cases were reported in Istanbul and Iskenderun between 2021 and 2022).

5. POLITICS AND SOCIETY

In the context of the country's current economic situation and the increasingly clear polarization of the electorate, social and political tensions could persist in the short and medium term. In Istanbul, protests can occur in areas around Taksim Square, Istiklal Street, and the districts of Besiktas, Beyoglu, and Kadikoy. More recently, protests have also been seen in Maltepe, Sisli, and Okmeydani.

In Ankara, however, protests are frequently concentrated in the central district of Kizilay. Protests are often not authorized by the national authorities, thus resulting in even violent intervention by the police if they occur. In the south-east of the country, there are frequent protests and street demonstrations, including violent ones, organized by the Kurdish minority. The risk of social unrest increases significantly in the case of Turkish military operations against Kurdish groups in Syria. On the foreign policy front, there are reports of tensions between Turkey and the government of Syria due to Turkish support for some of the rebel groups in the country. Ankara also maintains a strong presence in Libya, where it intervened in the past alongside the Tripoli authorities against Khalifa Haftar's Libyan National Army (LNA), supported among others by Egypt and Russia. In light of the persistence of a state of instability and possible tensions between the foreign powers involved in Libya, arrests or sanctions of an economic nature towards individuals, institutions, or interests attributable to these countries cannot be ruled out. Relations between Turkey and Greece remain unstable due to disputes between the two countries over managing the migration crisis and controlling waters in the

Aegean and Mediterranean. Such disputes can result in in-depth checks and arbitrary detentions of vessels transiting the maritime areas subject to dispute between the two countries. The outbreak of the conflict in the Gaza Strip (7 October 2023) has led to a deterioration of the complex relations between Turkey and Israel. Initially moderate, Ankara's position towards the Israeli state has become increasingly intransigent in parallel with the worsening of the crisis and the humanitarian situation in the Strip. As a result, Israel has called on its citizens present in Türkiye to leave the country.

6. ETHICS

Corruption is a widespread phenomenon in both the public and private sectors. Requests for bribes are frequent, especially in the public procurement and construction sectors. In terms of human rights, a general increase in the repression of political dissent has been reported, which has especially affected both Turkish and foreign workers in the information sector. The Turkish government is approving an increasingly stringent policy on the control of social networks and the internet. The Turkish authorities are able to have information on users and content shared via social media (Twitter, Facebook, Instagram, etc.) thanks to a recent law approved by the Turkish Parliament. Companies that fail to cooperate with Turkish authorities may face administrative sanctions and potentially have their services suspended indefinitely.

7. TRANSPORT

We recommend consulting the visa section on the Turkish Ministry of Foreign Affairs website for information on the documentation necessary to enter the country. The visa procedure can be carried out as outlined by consulting the EVisa website. Anyone traveling to Turkey must be in possession of a passport with a validity of at least 60 days beyond the expiry date of the visa or residence permit.

7.1 Air Transport

It should be noted that until at least January 2024, Turkey has closed its airspace to all flights to and from Sulaymaniyah International Airport (ISU), Iraq, following an alleged increase in PKK activities at the stopover. Consequently, there could be cancellations of flights to the airport in question in the coming weeks. At the same time, the Turkish government closed the national airspace to some flights operated by Armenian airlines, particularly those connecting Armenia to third destinations. We recommend that you check the status of your flight with your airline. At the beginning of April 2019, the New Istanbul International Airport (IST) entered full operation, replacing the Ataturk International Airport for commercial traffic. Another airport - Sabiha Gökçen - is located in the Asian part of the city.

Strong security measures at airports reduce, but do not eliminate, the risks of possible attacks. In the past, there have been some cases of plane hijackings, almost all on domestic routes, which ended with the capture or killing of the hijacker and without harm to the passengers. To keep up to date on the reliability of airlines, you can consult the European Commission's multilingual website.

7.2 Road Routes

Driving is on the right. For citizens of some European countries, their national driving license is sufficient to get behind the wheel; in all other cases, an international driving license is required. The permitted blood alcohol level is 0.05%. For excess speed and/or driving while intoxicated or following drug consumption, the license will be withdrawn (generally for 6 months), and a ban on driving on Turkish territory for a variable period. The rate of road accidents is quite high, and local drivers' driving style is aggressive and not very disciplined.

In the event of an accident, it is mandatory to wait for the police to arrive. If you incur a fine, please remember that the vehicle may be subject to seizure until the amount due has been paid. It is risky to travel throughout the south-east of the country. In addition to the borders with Syria, Iraq (where very high-security risks remain), Iran, and Armenia, there is the presence of Kurdish guerrillas, drug traffickers, and minefields (in most cases reported). Taxis available in the country's main urban centers are inexpensive and numerous. The availability of vehicles, however, is limited during rush hours. The metro service is active in the main cities of the country.

Turkey has a good railway network, with high-speed lines connecting some main cities (Istanbul, Ankara, Eskisehir, and Konya). A temporary military restriction zone has been established in the Mount Ararat area, to which access is not permitted except with a special permit; other temporary military restriction zones have been established in the eastern provinces. Do not use the bus service for travel.

8. Safety Precautions

The entire south-eastern area presents a more critical security situation than the rest of the country. Therefore, any trips to these areas must be carried out after a specific analysis to identify and mitigate the specific critical issues.

- In case of travel, especially in the most at-risk areas, it is recommended to adopt appropriate safety measures and request the support of expert personnel.
- Upon arrival at the airport, where contact with a specific person has not already been foreseen, pay attention to those who approach and offer themselves as companions to reach the destination in question or for any other reason.
- Choose large chain hotels or, if not available, find out in advance which structures should be avoided.

- In hotels, always find out about the emergency exit closest to your room and the route to reach it.

- Make sure you always have a charged and functioning mobile phone with you, which has emergency numbers to contact in case of need that have been previously stored.

- If renting a car with a driver for urban and extra-urban travel is necessary, use only reliable personnel verified by the company or provided by proven agencies.

- When traveling in eastern and south-eastern Anatolia, it is advisable, if possible, to travel along the main roads and avoid traveling after sunset.

- Pay particular attention when driving at night in rural areas because agricultural vehicles often have no lights.

- Remember that in the event of a road accident, it is mandatory to wait for the police to arrive for investigations.

- Pay particular attention to the presence of mines along the borders with Syria, Armenia, Iraq, and Iran.

- Always carry with you a working mobile phone with a charged battery, on which the emergency numbers and who to contact in case of need have been stored in advance.

- In consideration of the terrorist risk, it is appropriate to stay informed about any deterioration in security conditions and the related increase in the risk level, also following the authorities' press releases, and strictly follow safety procedures throughout your stay in the country; if you come across suspicious people, attitudes or objects, inform the security forces as soon as possible and quickly leave the area and inform the authorities, possibly getting the assistance of a company representative or a trusted contact; in the event of evacuation of a building due to a terrorist alarm, head to a safe place, avoiding staying outside the same building, due to the risk of attacks directed explicitly against the people evacuated.

- Avoid, if possible, passing or stopping for long periods near political-institutional buildings, military bases, police stations, and religious buildings because they are potential targets of terrorist actions.

- For security reasons, it is preferable not to reveal the name of the company you work for unless necessary. In this regard, we recommend removing any labels and logos from your luggage or clothing.

- Adopt basic precautions to prevent petty crime: monitor bags, suitcases, and valuables; keep your bag on the inside of the sidewalk; in case of payments by credit card, personally supervise the operation (to avoid the risk of cloning); do not display money, jewels or other valuable objects in public; do not carry documents and valuables in one place (e.g., back pocket, bag); be aware of what is happening around you, not being distracted by seemingly random incidents; leave unnecessary documents and money in a safe, take with you a copy of your travel and identity documents (including a copy of your passport and the relevant page with the entry visa, if applicable); do not resist in the event of a mugging and do not react in the event of a robbery.

- To reduce the risk of computer scams, thefts, robberies, and sudden kidnappings, adopt standard precautions when operating ATMs. In particular, it is advisable to pay attention to any suspicious people;

- Do not withdraw large amounts of money; do not accept help from strangers during the withdrawal phase; do not use apparently tampered ATMs; cover the PIN code entry with one hand.

- In relation to data protection, the following precautionary measures are recommended: before leaving, equip yourself with all the firmware and software updates suggested by your system, regardless of whether you bring your own personal device or the one provided by the company (the and outdated platforms are more vulnerable to cyber attacks); bring with you only the data necessary for business meetings; store the data on one or more mobile drives (duly encrypted or equipped with a secure password) rather than on a laptop or tablet (this way, in the event of an accident, it will still be possible to recover all the data); always use your own VPN (Virtual Private Network) and do not connect to public Wi-Fi networks (airports, stations, etc.), as a very low level of security generally characterizes them. Pay maximum attention to the confidentiality of company information.

- Regarding the use of Social Media, during a business trip, it is advisable to keep a low profile and not publish personal information (e.g., photographs depicting your plane ticket or passport) to avoid identity theft. We also recommend that you don't post personal or inappropriate comments about your mission.

- Do not approach any gatherings to avoid the risk of being involved in potential clashes. Do not try to force protesters' blocks or pickets, as this could provoke violent reactions.

- At checkpoints, remain calm and alert. Promptly comply with the requests of soldiers and policemen to prevent the latter from reacting.

- In addition to the precautions indicated above, women are advised, among other things, to ignore unwanted attention;

- Unless strictly necessary, do not go out or travel alone at night, and above all, avoid isolated, poorly lit, infamous, or degraded areas.

- Please remember that the possession, sale, and export of ancient objects is against the law and can lead to prison sentences of 5 to 12 years, in addition to a hefty fine.

- In the event of an earthquake, it is advisable to adopt the following measures. If you are inside a building, seek shelter in a doorway, near a load-bearing wall, under a table, or under a beam; stay away from windows, glass, or unanchored structures (bookcases, shelves, cabinets, etc.); be careful when using the stairs (they are the weakest parts of the building) and elevators (they could get stuck). If you are outside, keep away from trees, poles, walls, damaged buildings, power lines, industrial plants, lakes, and beaches (tsunami waves may occur). By car, stop along the side of the road and wait for the shaking to stop, avoiding stopping along overpasses, bridges, and elevated roads and highways. In all cases, remain calm, follow the instructions in the emergency plans, and wait for help. Keep in mind that a strong earthquake is usually followed by a series of aftershocks. It is also advisable to leave telephone lines and roads clear so as not to hinder rescue operations.

- To purchase a Turkish telephone card (SIM), you must request (through the telephone operator) the registration of your mobile phone number with the Turkish Telecommunications Authority to avoid automatic blocking. You must have your passport when registering.

- It is generally possible to make payments with the main international currencies (dollars and euros) or with credit cards, except in smaller shops or taxis.

- The use of travelers' checks is possible. ATMs are common; for their exact location, it is possible to consult the websites of the VISA Circuit and the Mastercard Circuit.

- In Turkey, the main mobile operators are Turkcell, Turk Telekom, and Vodafone, which provide data connections on 3G and 4G networks. To check their network coverage, you can consult the Open Signal website.

9. Cultural Indications

Please note that Turkish authorities and society are generally intolerant towards the LGBTQ+ community. The regulatory references relating to "crimes against public morality," "family protection," 11 Travel Guide and "unnatural sexual behavior" are sometimes used for legal and police actions both against individuals and against associations dealing with the theme.

- o Avoid publicly dealing with issues such as Kurdish separatism, the Armenian question, and, more generally, the current political and economic situation of the country; refrain from comments or actions that could be interpreted as an offense to the figure of Mustafa Kemal Ataturk (founding father of the Republic of Turkey) or to the nation; during Ramadan celebrations, avoid drinking, eating or smoking in public, from dawn to dusk.

- o Do not take photos of sensitive areas and installations and show respect towards state symbols, especially the flag; any comment considered offensive towards the Turkish nation or any act against the national flag or currency is punishable by a prison sentence of between 6 months and 3 years.

o   For female staff, covering clothing is recommended in the more conservative areas (particularly in the south-east of the country), and paying attention to Islamic norms, culture, and sensitivities is essential. In the main urban centers, it is possible to dress according to Western standards but avoid excessively flashy clothing. Harassment of foreign women is generally verbal, while sexual violence is rare, except in the less safe neighborhoods of Istanbul.

o   Business meetings are generally formal, so it is advisable to wear appropriate clothing.

10. Business Information

Business cards are typically exchanged after presentations.

*   It is advisable to always call the other party by their professional title. In the absence of a professional title, using "bey" for men and "hanem" for women is better.

*   It is advisable to make appointments in advance and ask for confirmation of the time on the same day.

*   Before addressing the topics on the agenda, it is preferable to start with informal conversations to establish a climate of mutual trust. Typically, tea or coffee is offered first.

Negotiations can be slower than in other countries. Hospitality in Türkiye is a significant value.

- MAIN HOLIDAYS IN THE COUNTRY in 2024 (Excluding New Year's Eve):

- 23 April, National Sovereignty and Children's Day;

- May 1st, Work and Solidarity Day;

- May 19, Atatürk Commemoration and Youth and Sports Day;

- 15 July Day of Democracy and National Unity;

- August 30, Victory Day;

- 28-29 October, Republic Day. Added to these are the Islamic religious holidays:

- 9-12 April, Ramazan Bayrami (end of Ramadan); 15-19 June, Kurban Bayrami (feast of sacrifice).

CHAPTER 9: CONCLUSIONS

As I described earlier in Chapter 1, Italy, in the "packaging" sector, construction of automatic packaging machine lines, is the first in the world with its 10 billion turnover with 85% of exports for a simple fact: it is a sector where craftsmanship, imagination and inventiveness still reign supreme.

Furthermore, there are many other sectors, such as:

Glasses

Classic footwear

Pharmaceutical specialties

Goldsmith, jewelry, and costume

Motorcycles and electric bicycles

Leather goods and luggage

Non-ferrous metal processing

Pharmaceutical raw materials

Microelectronics and components

Machines and plants for metallurgy, etc.

As a result, several tens of thousands of technicians, salespeople, and officials work on assignments in the most remote countries, not to mention all the NGO volunteers or university doctoral students abroad. This situation could be a big problem if something happens to whoever is responsible, be it a company, a university, or an NGO.

I have often put myself in the shoes of employees, especially young people who agree to go on business trips to supplement their salary, unaware of the risks they run without being informed and trained by the companies. Not even being aware of a procedure at the arrival airport to verify the true identity of those who are waiting for you.

I find it disgraceful that many companies do not organize training and information courses for their employees and do not analyze the situation of where their employees will work through a country form. Who knows if one day some politician will propose some amendment to Legislative Decree 81/2008 in order to make it much clearer what the various steps a company must take to mitigate or eliminate exogenous risks.

The recognition and obligation of the figure of the ISO/UNI 10459 certified "security manager" and a UNI/PDR 124/22 updated "Travel Risk Manager".

12.9.2023 taking inspiration from ISO/UNI 31030. Another problem is the following:

As a company, I cannot take advantage of an armed escort abroad from a company registered in Italy, i.e., a PSC (private security company), because Italian law simply does not provide for them.

Therefore, in the 80 billion or more that the various PSCs invoice the world for, mostly the USA (46%), Great Britain (19%), and then France, Canada, South Africa, Australia, and the Middle East, Italy is totally excluded.

Another very important fact is linked to the issue of intelligence, and let me explain better: if an Italian company is forced to turn to a PSC of another country to organize the security of their employees abroad, automatically, all information on arrival/departure times, place of work, name, and type of customer is clearly transmitted to these foreign PSCs who in turn can pass the information on to our potential foreign competitors.

Currently, if an Italian wants to open a PSC, he must do so in Great Britain, USA, and France; consequently, these companies will pay taxes abroad.

Please refer to ISNN-075-1448 on this topic: "Private Military and Security Companies: The Italian Case in the International Context," by Esther Marchetti.

www.ingramcontent.com/pod-product-compliance
Lightning Source LLC
Chambersburg PA
CBHW051104050726
47592CB00002B/660